BLOOMING BEAUTIES
A Springtime Coloring Book For Adults

Copyright
copyright© 2024 created by Lovely Fancybookpress
All rights reserved.

Bibliographical Note
Blooming Beauties Coloring Book is a new work,
first published by Amazon, Inc, in 2024

International Standard Book Number
ISBN: 9798320605852

Manufactured in US

"Blooming Beauties: A Springtime Coloring Book For Adults" invites you into a realm of radiant beauty and natural splendor. Within its pages, you'll discover an enchanting collection of intricate illustrations featuring captivating women adorned in the vibrant colors of spring. Each portrait is delicately intertwined with blooming flowers, lush gardens, and chirping birds, celebrating the rejuvenation of nature in all its glory.

Let your creativity flourish as you bring these portraits to life with a kaleidoscope of colors, capturing the essence of springtime joy and renewal with every stroke of your coloring pen. Embrace the enchantment of the season and immerse yourself in the timeless charm of "Blooming Beauties."

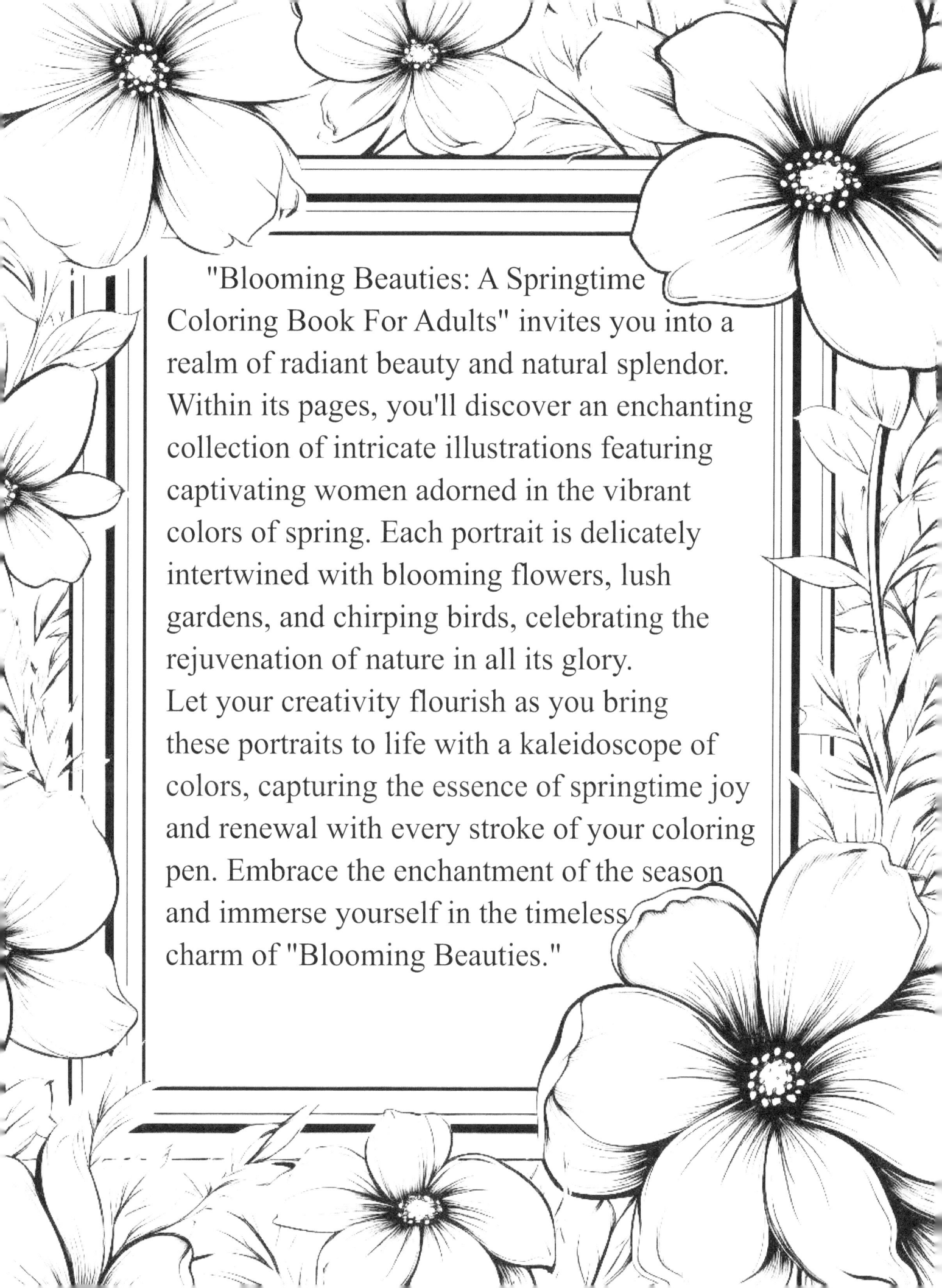

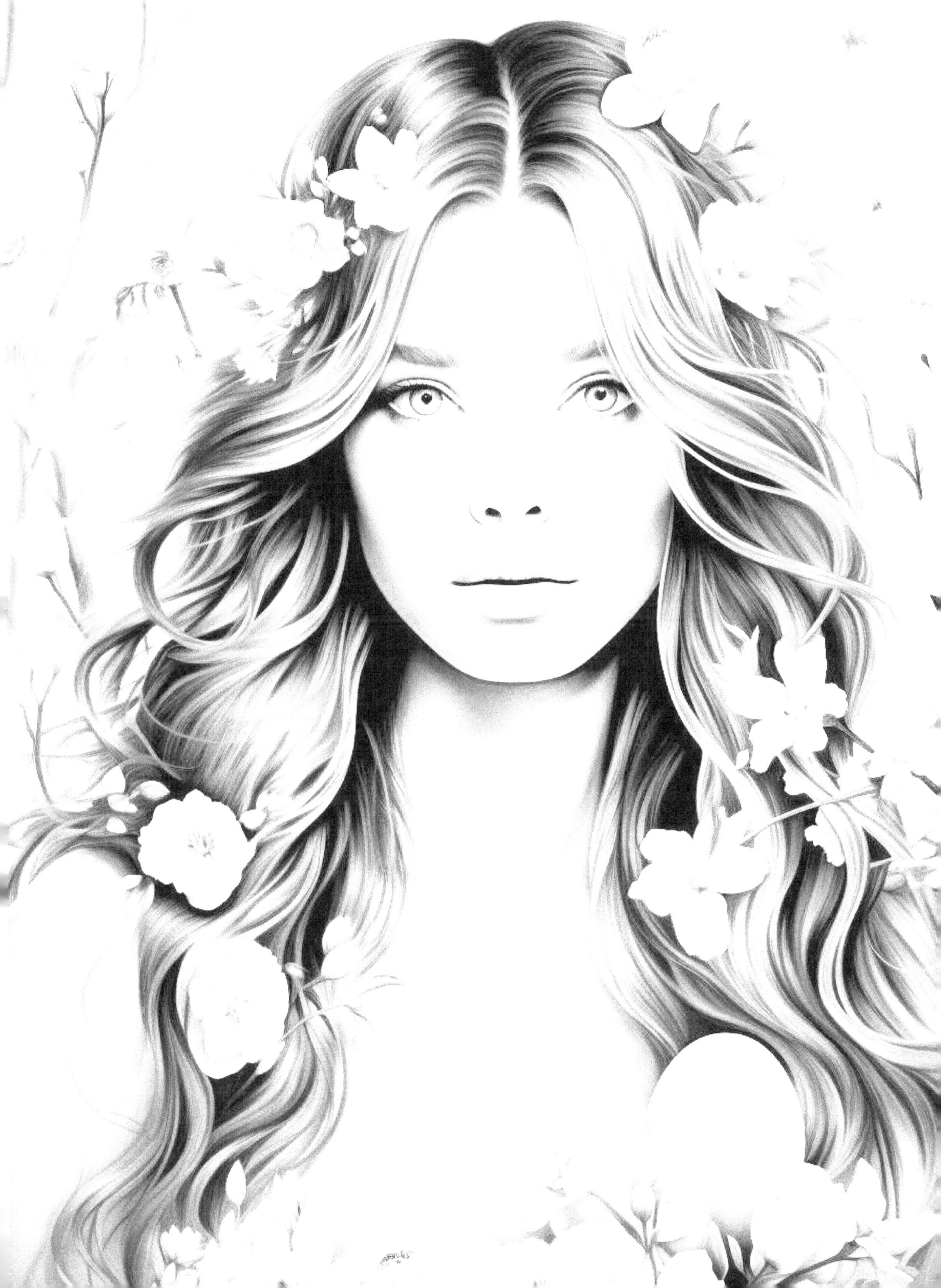

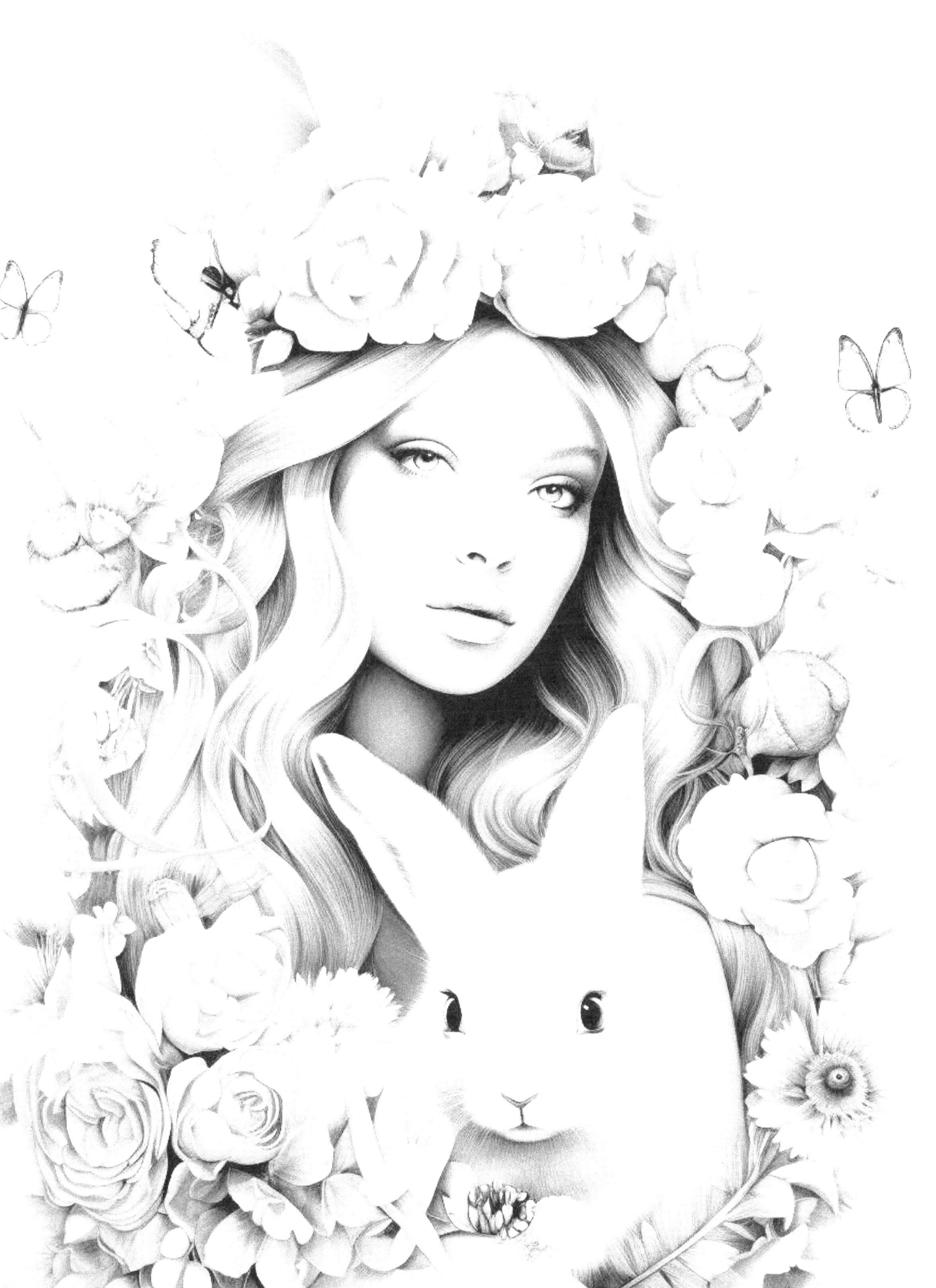

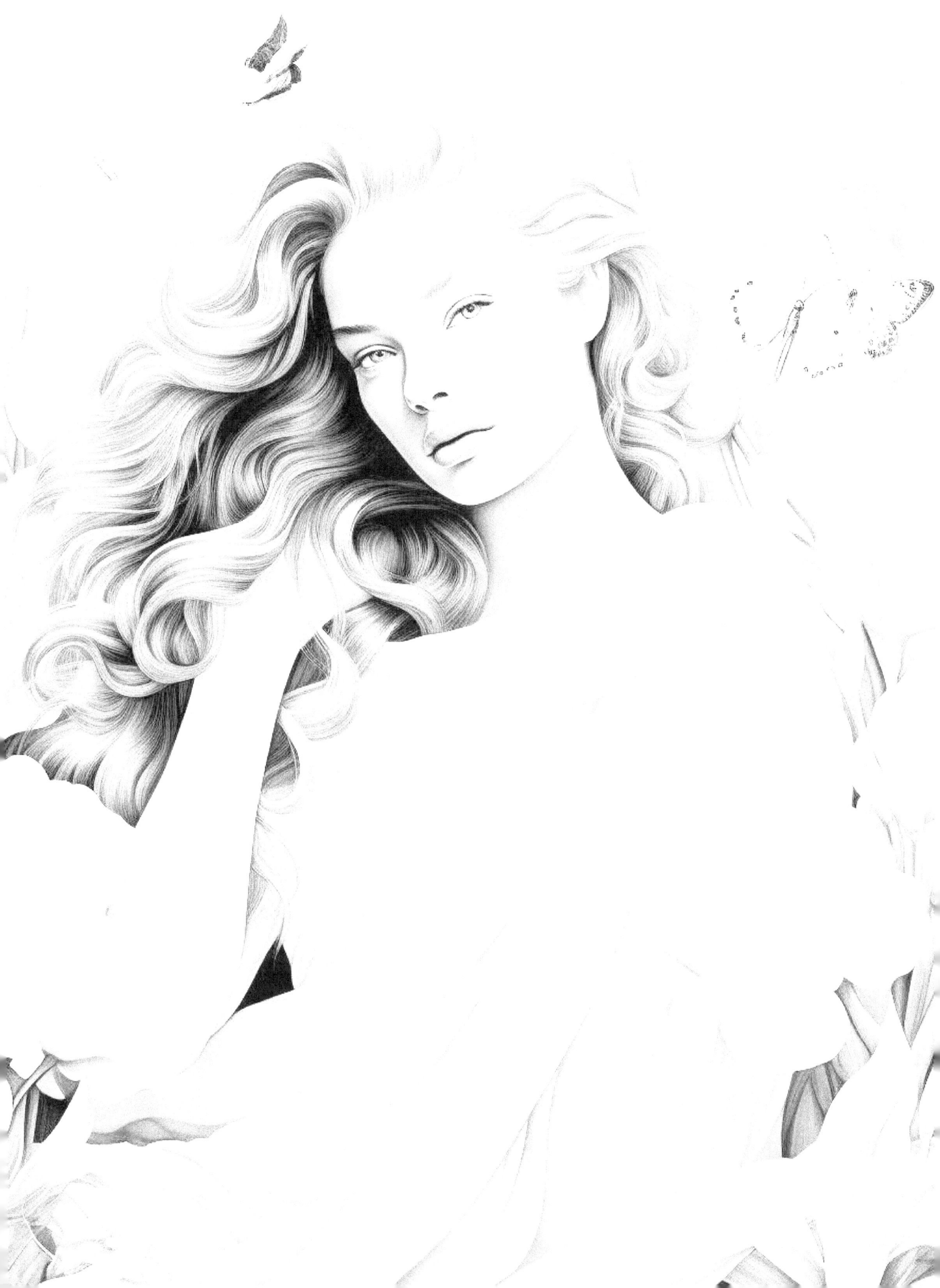

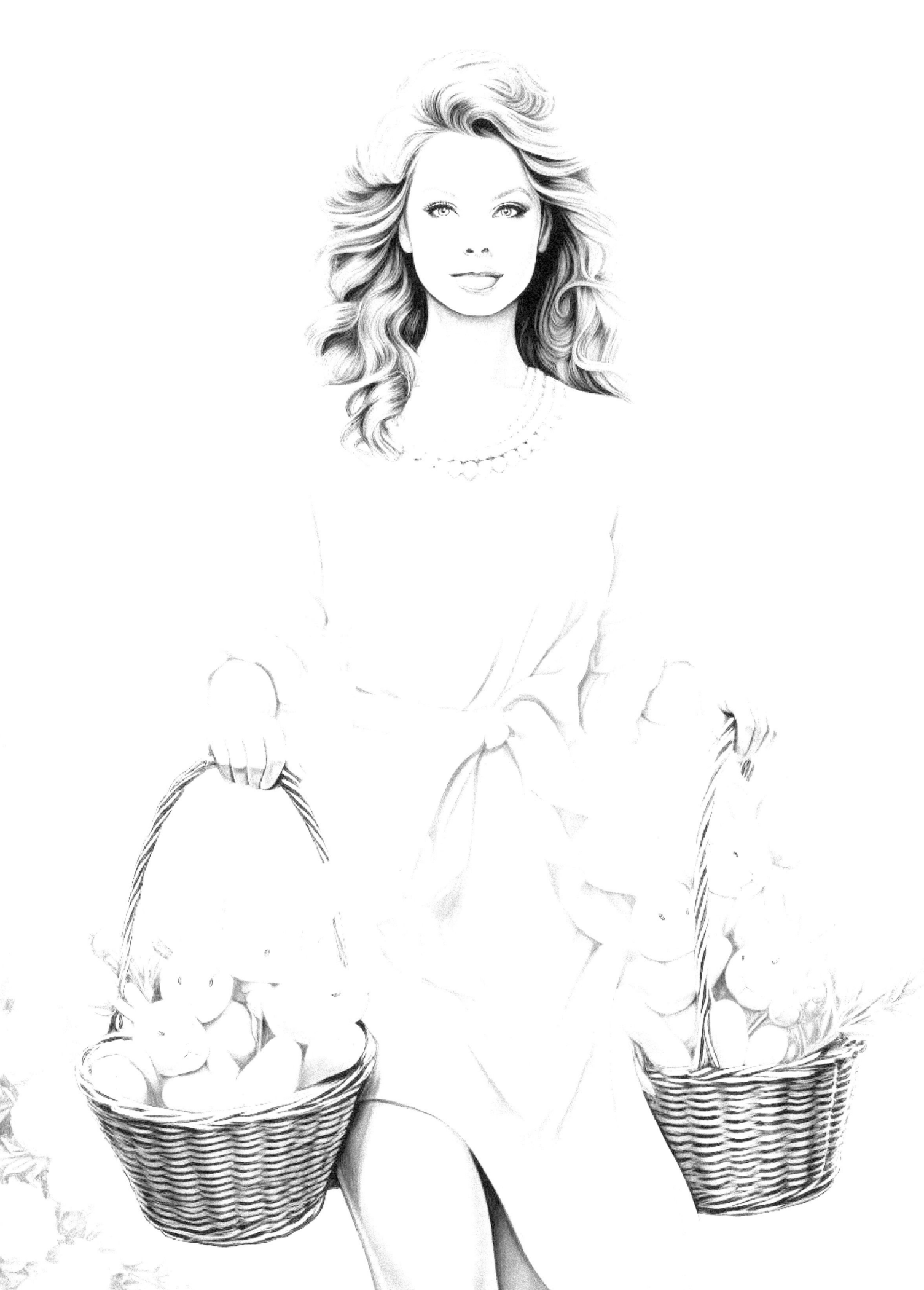

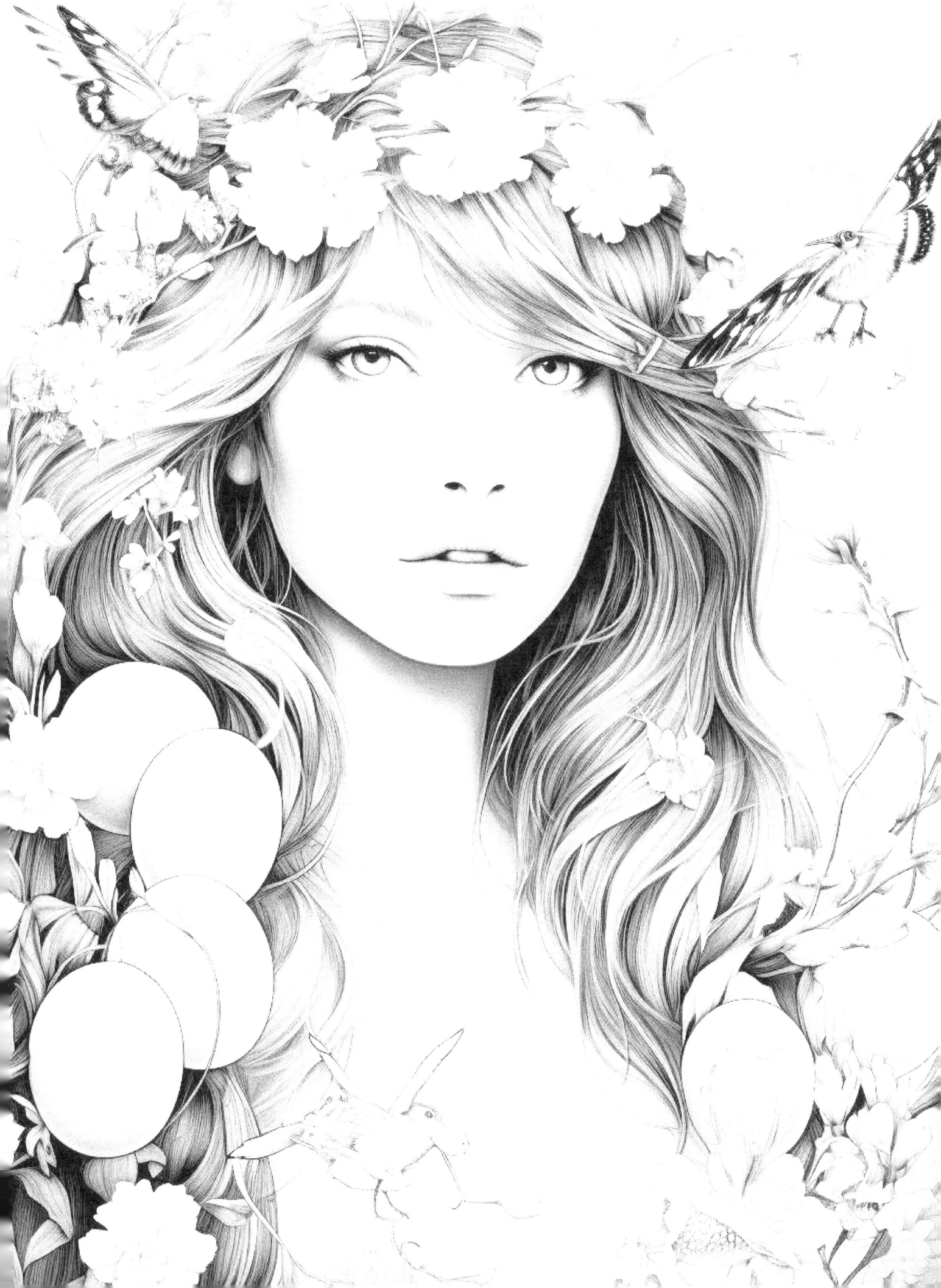

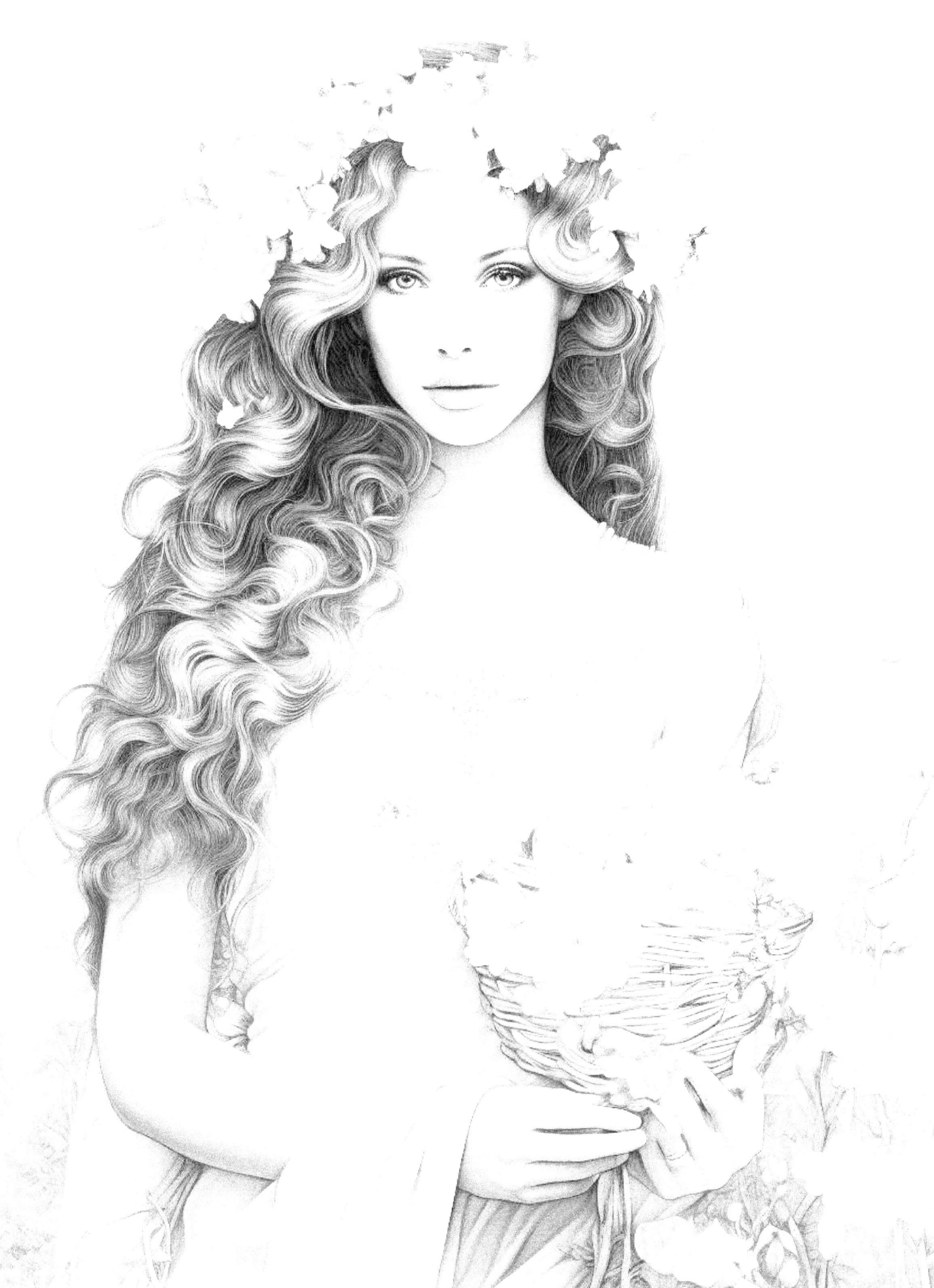

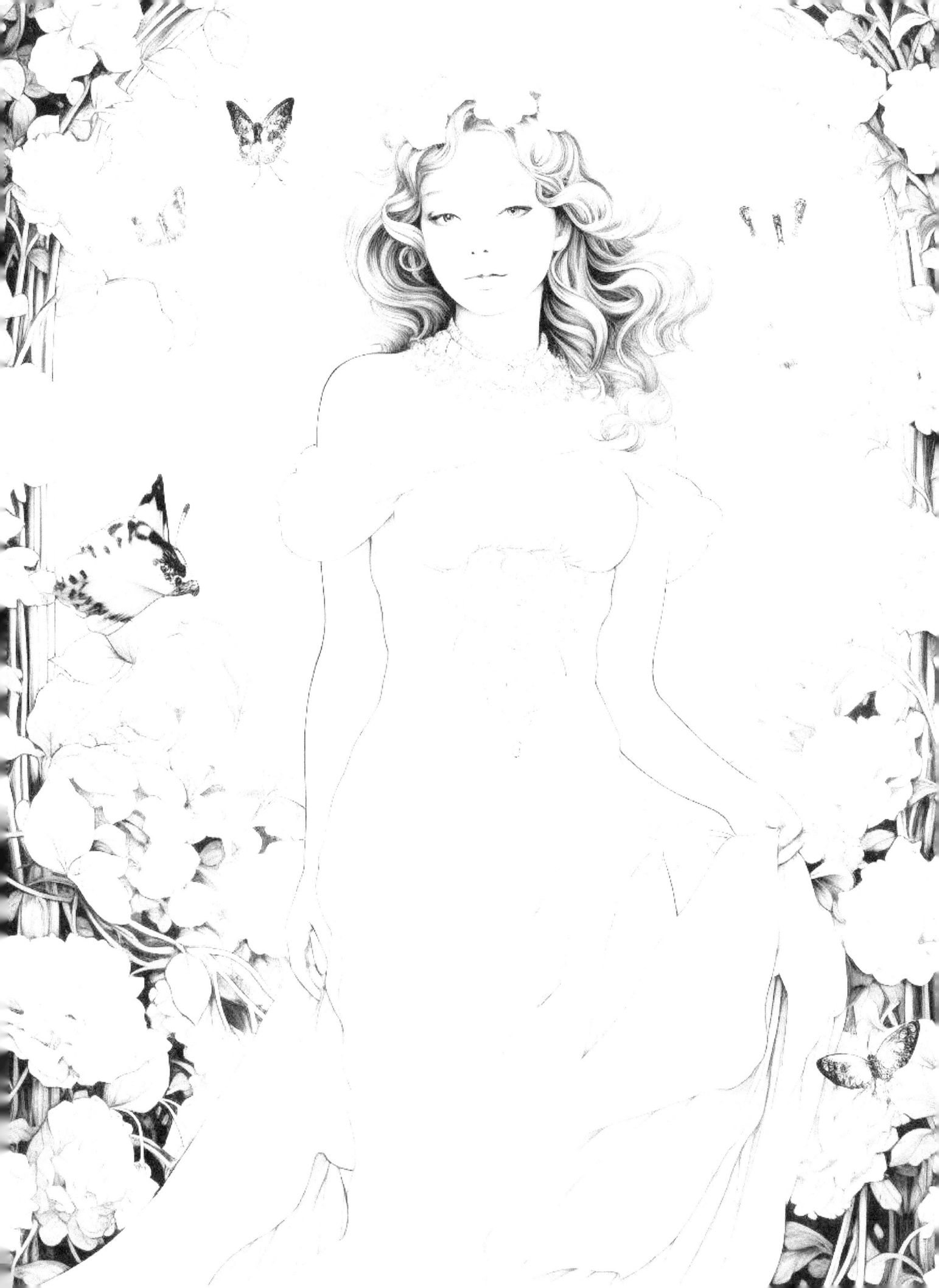

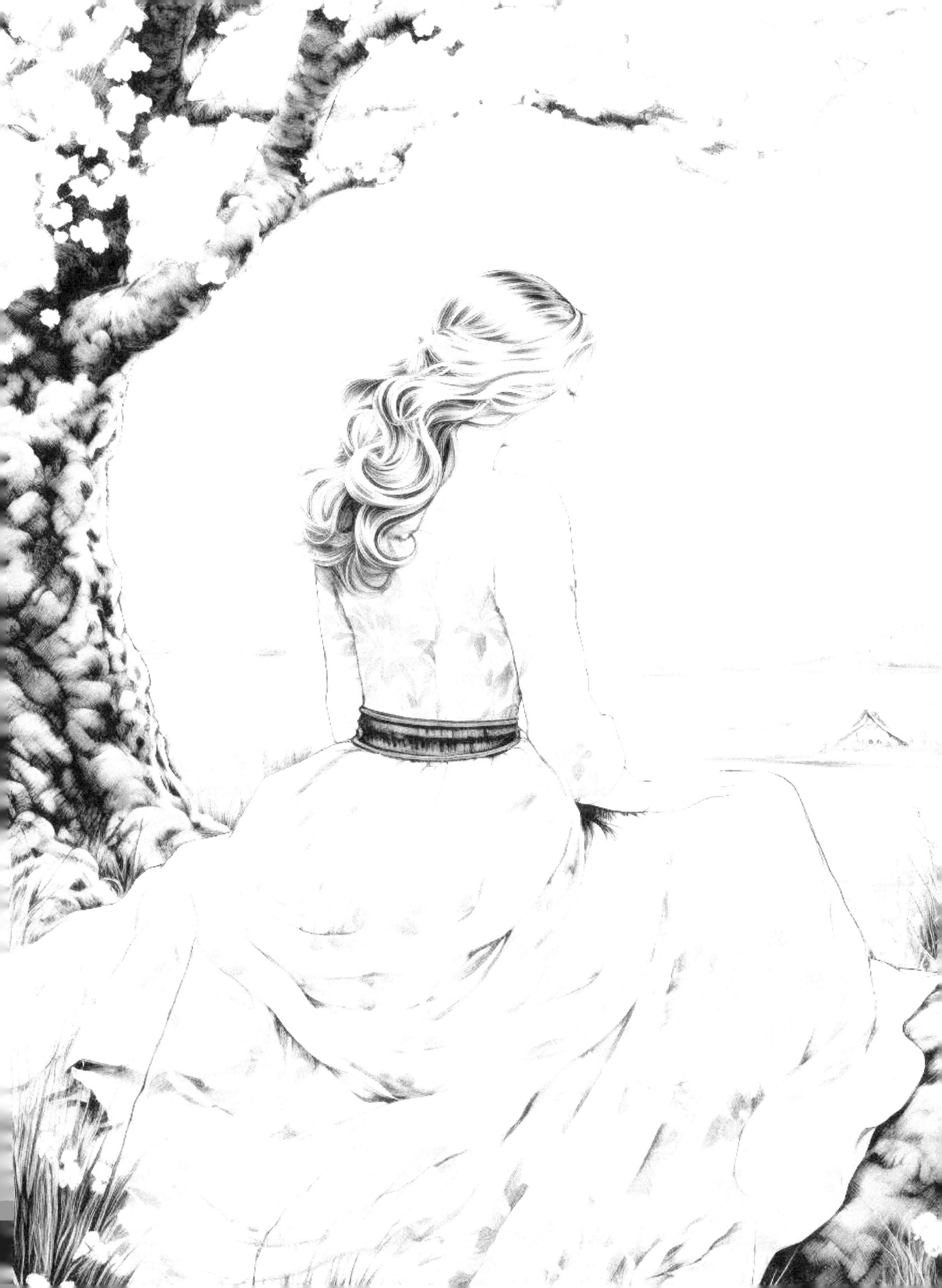

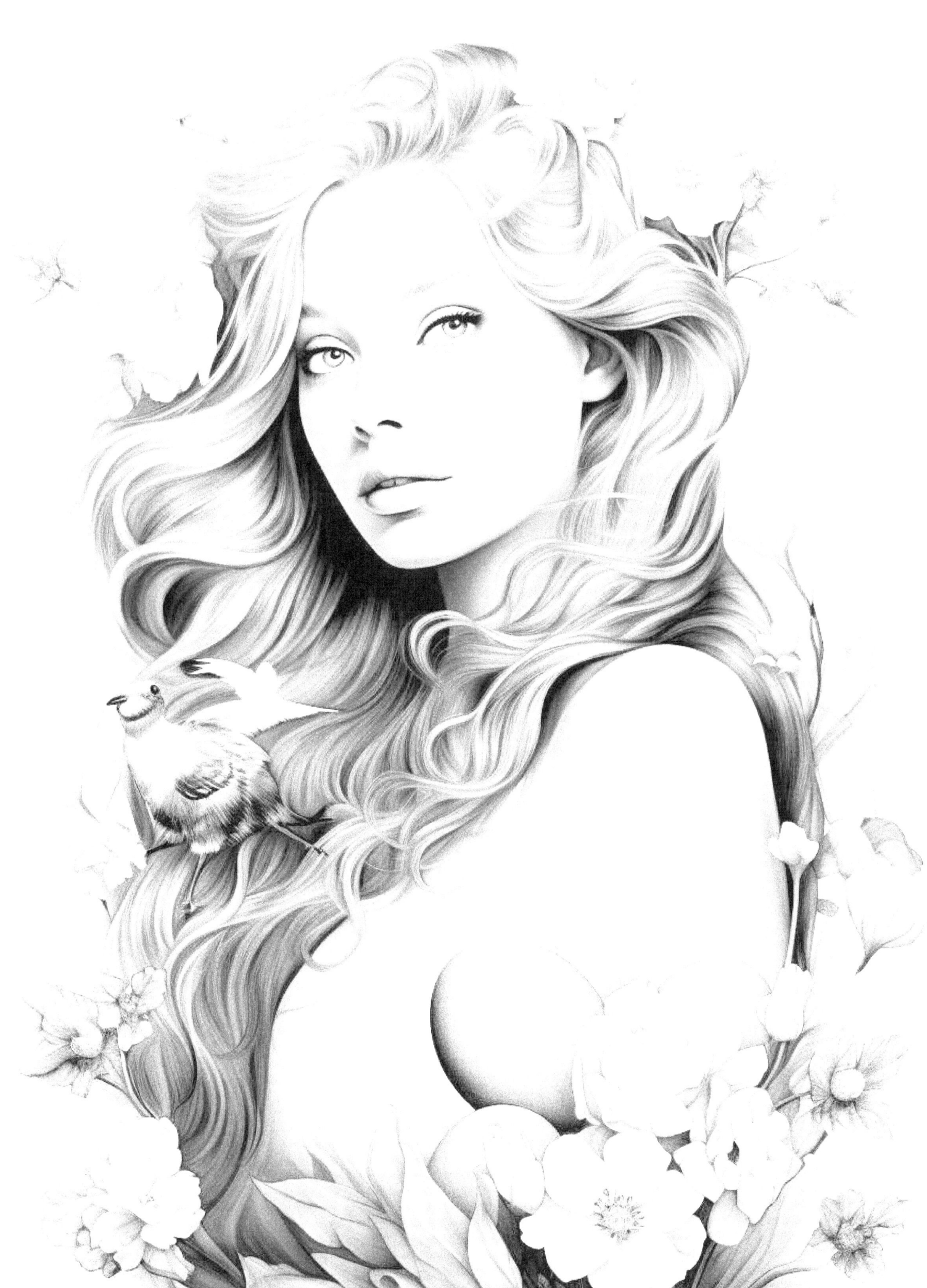

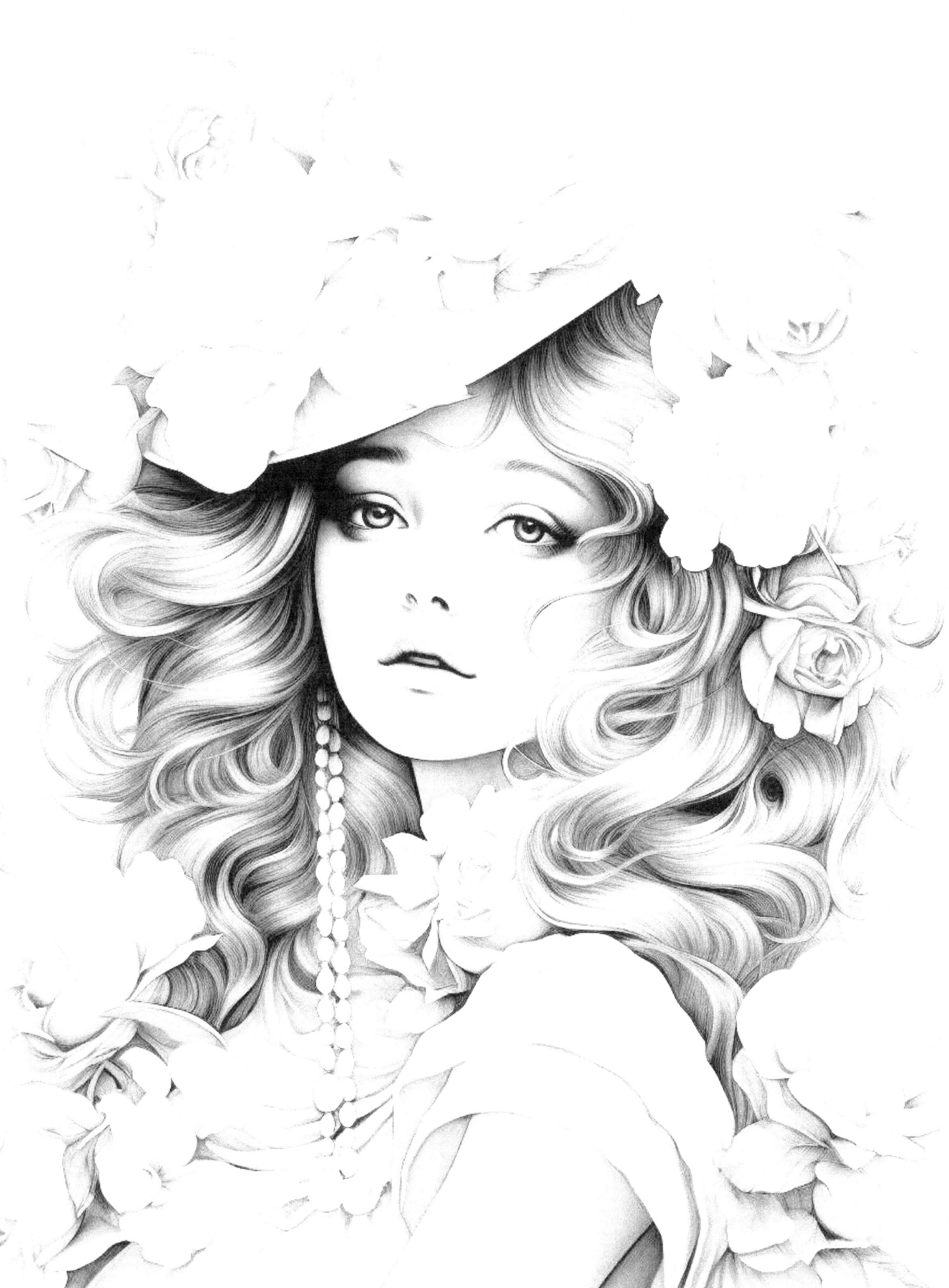

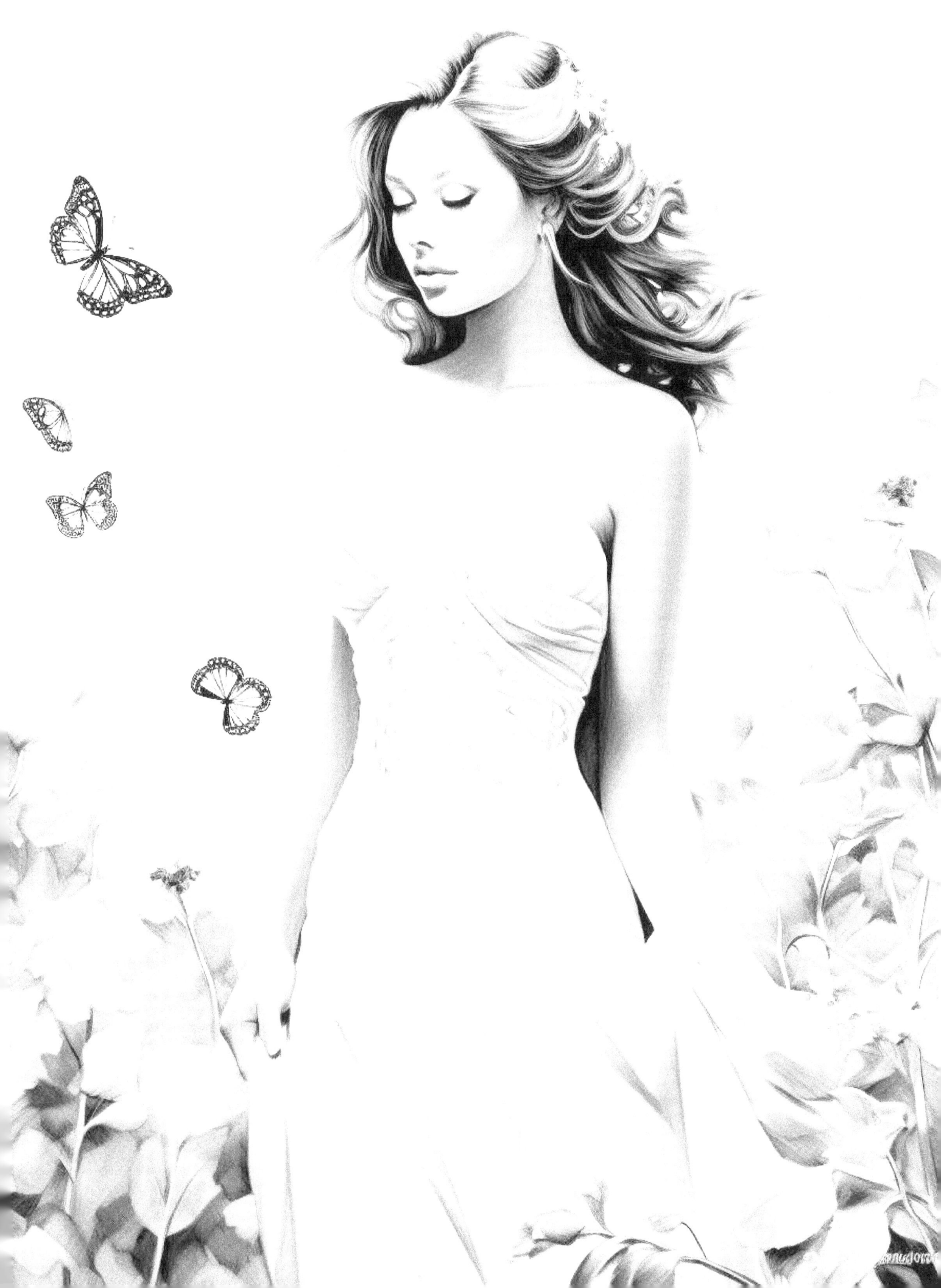

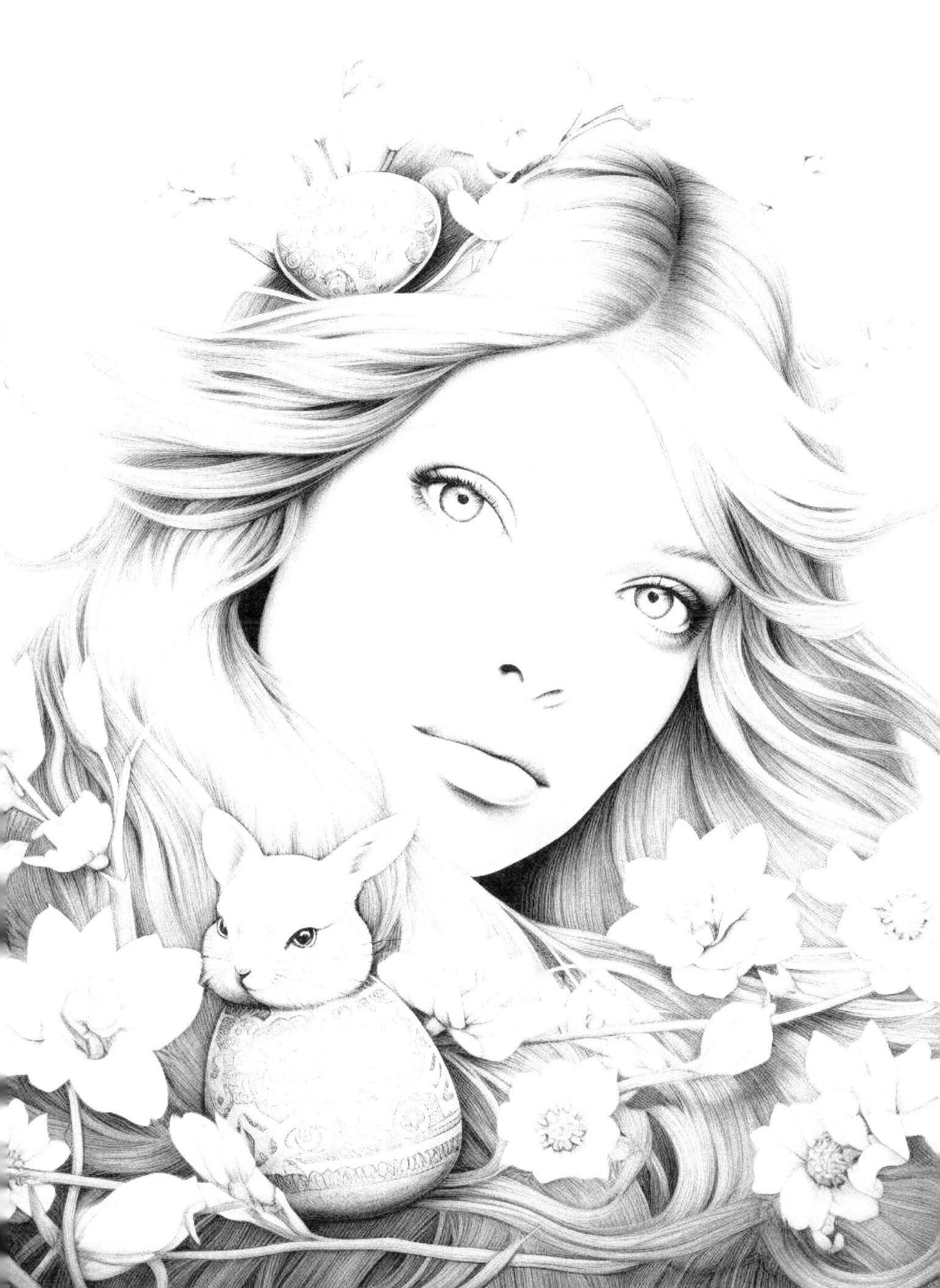

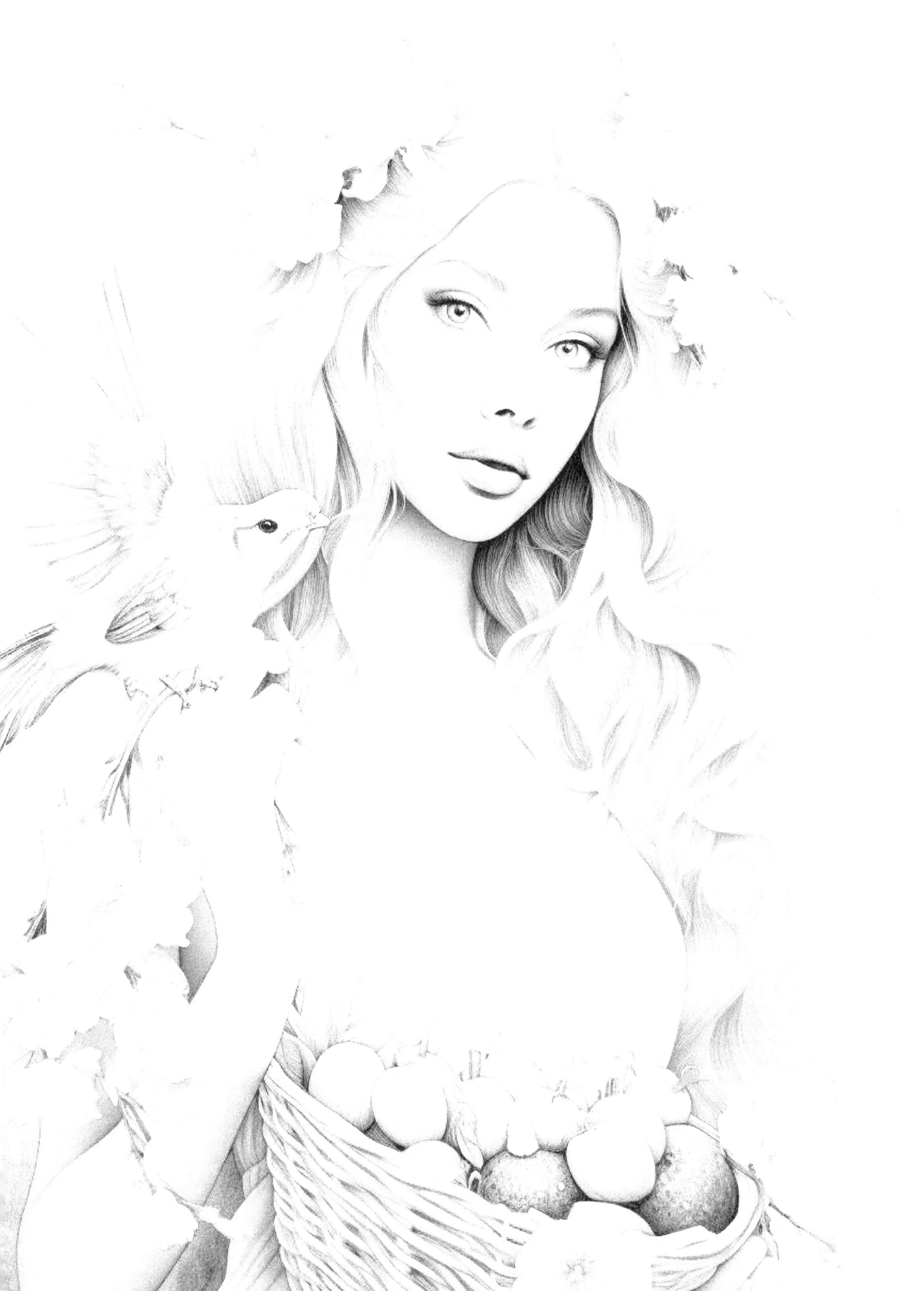

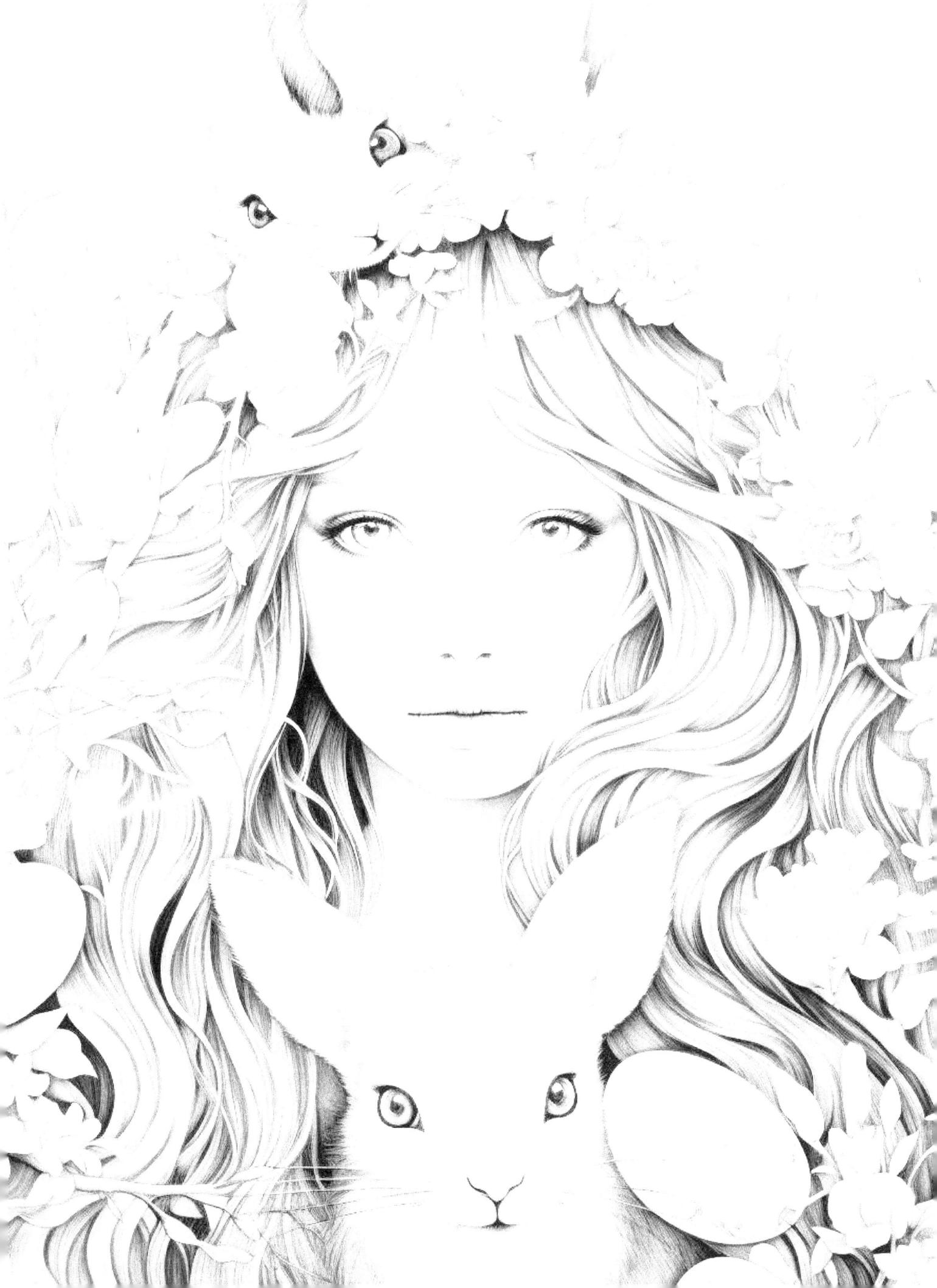

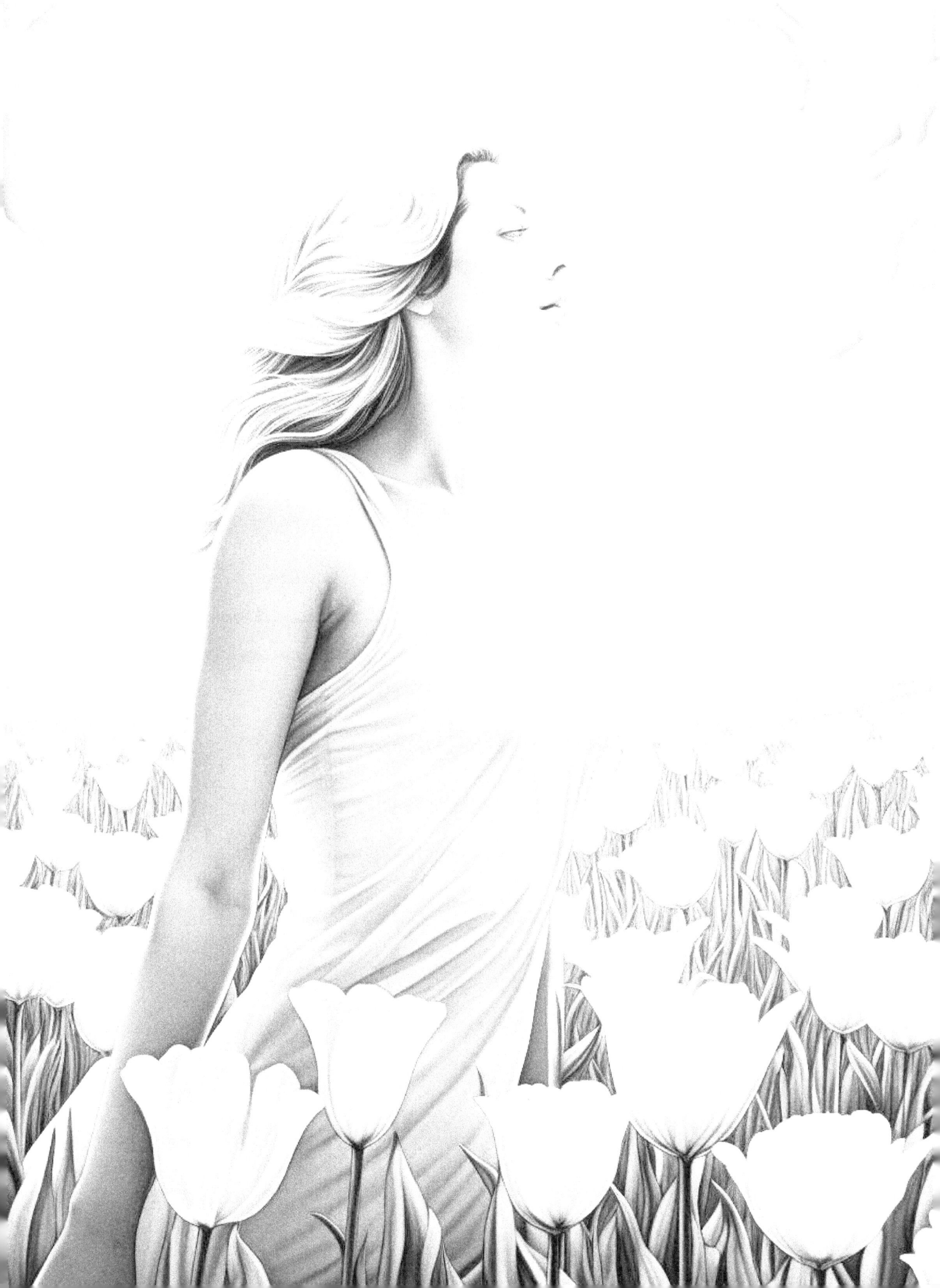

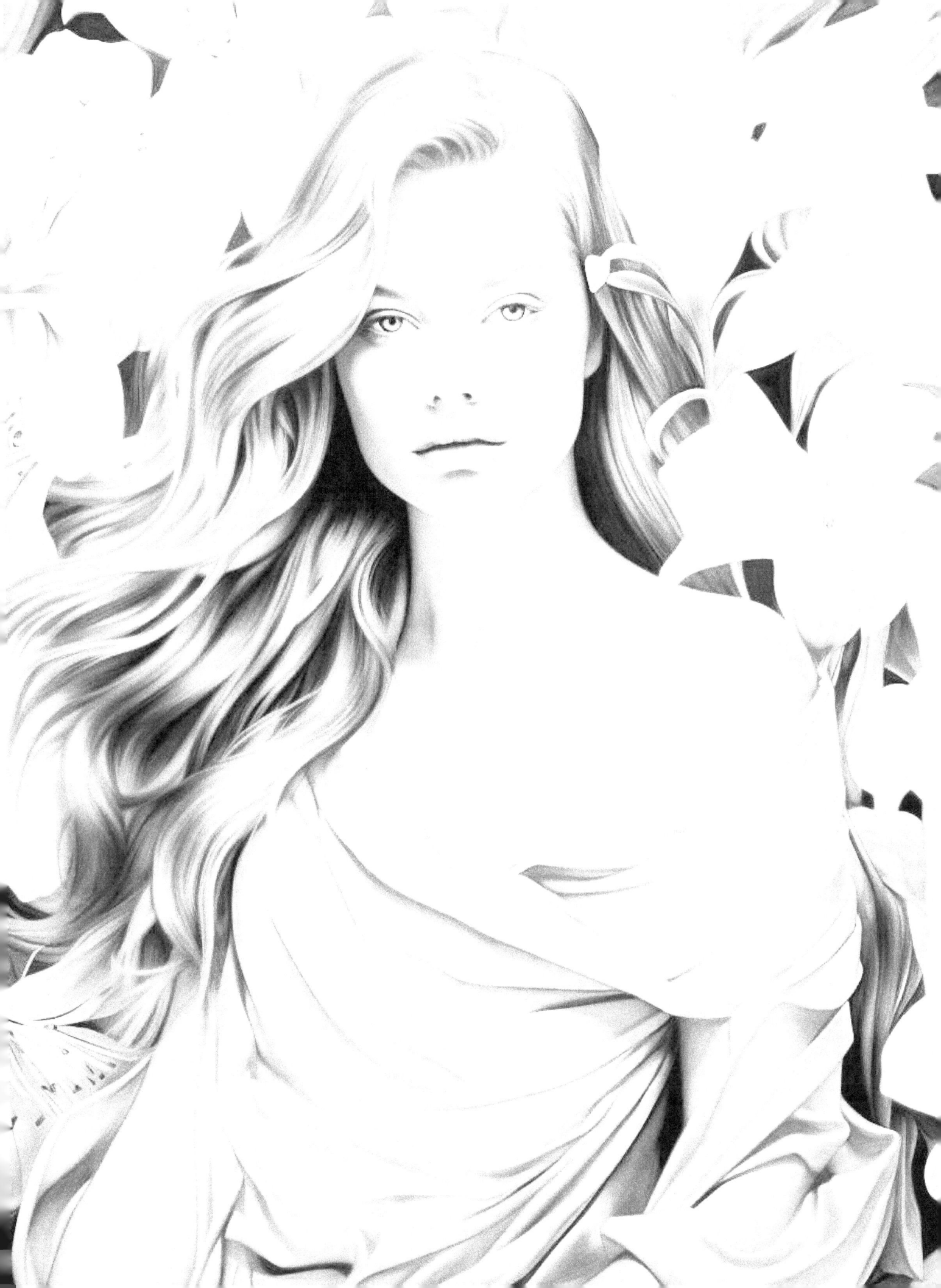

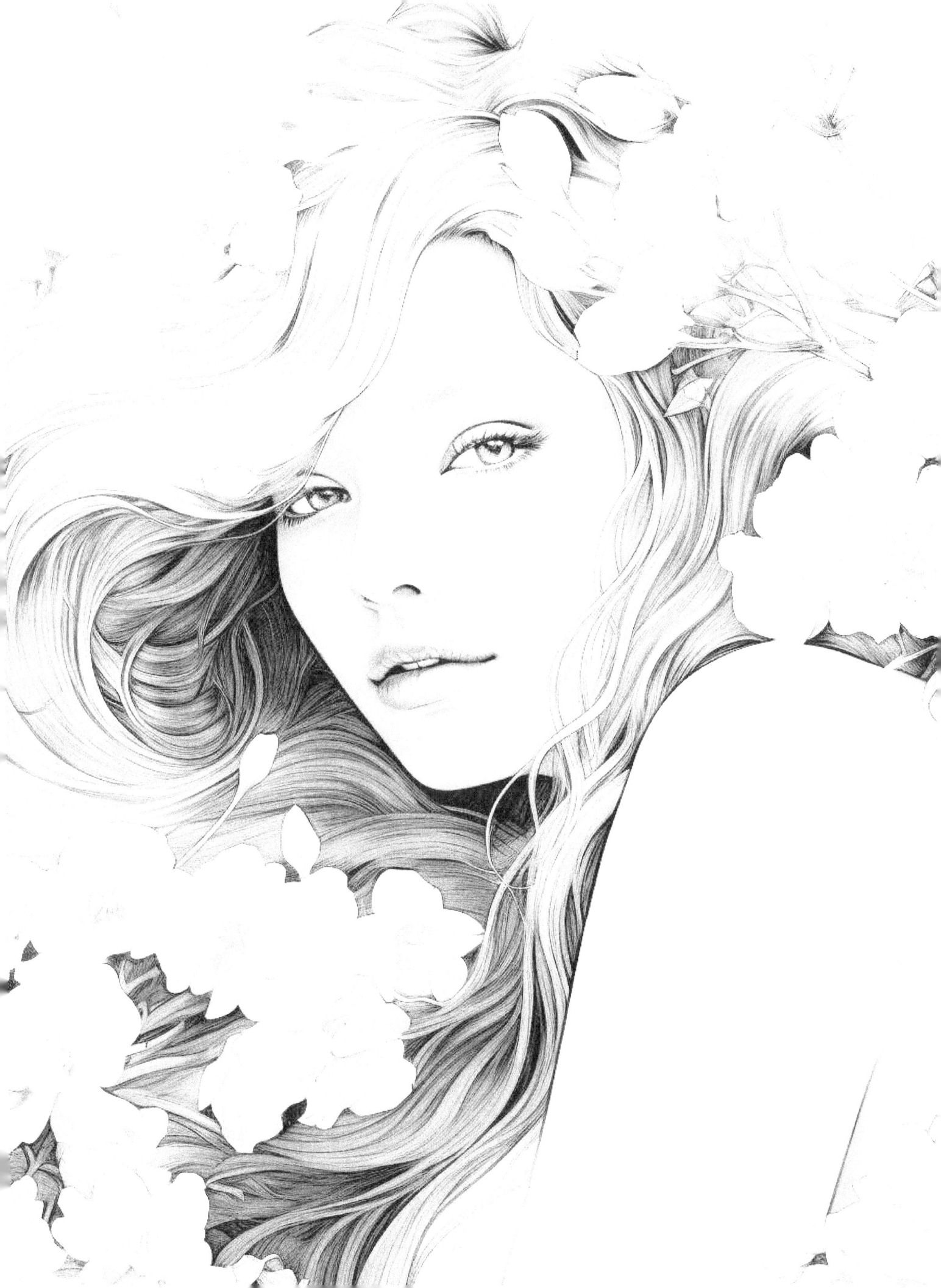

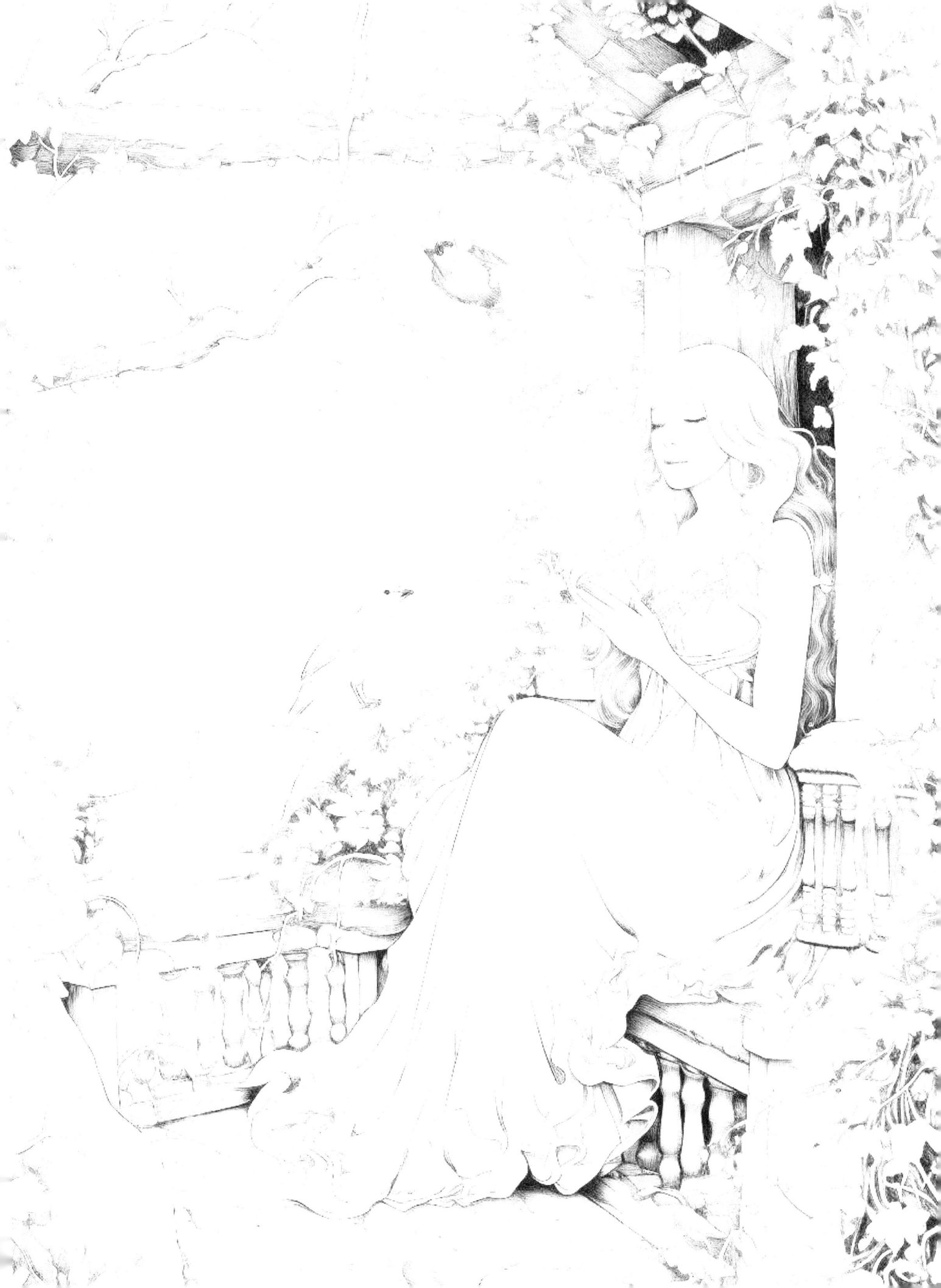

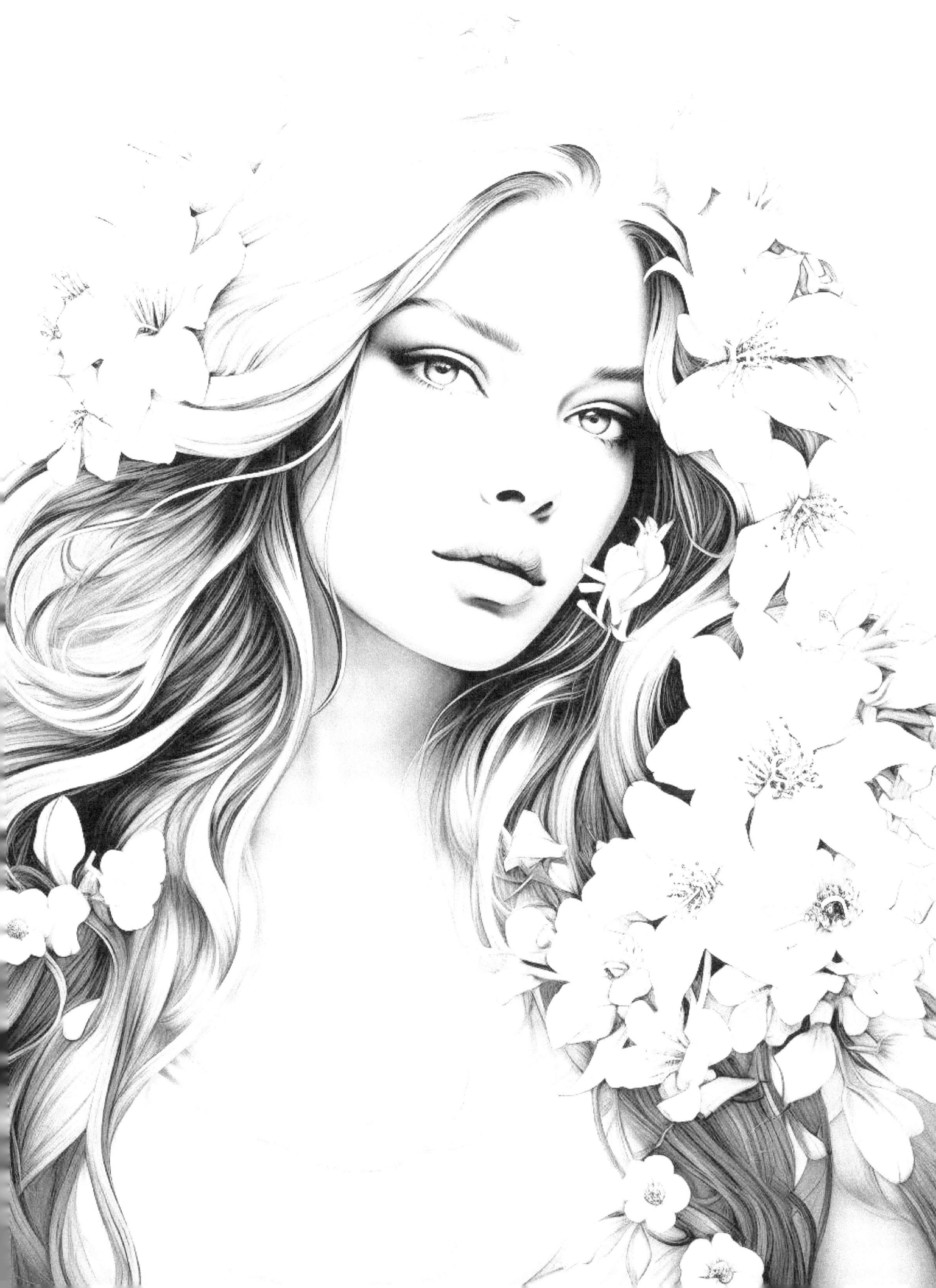

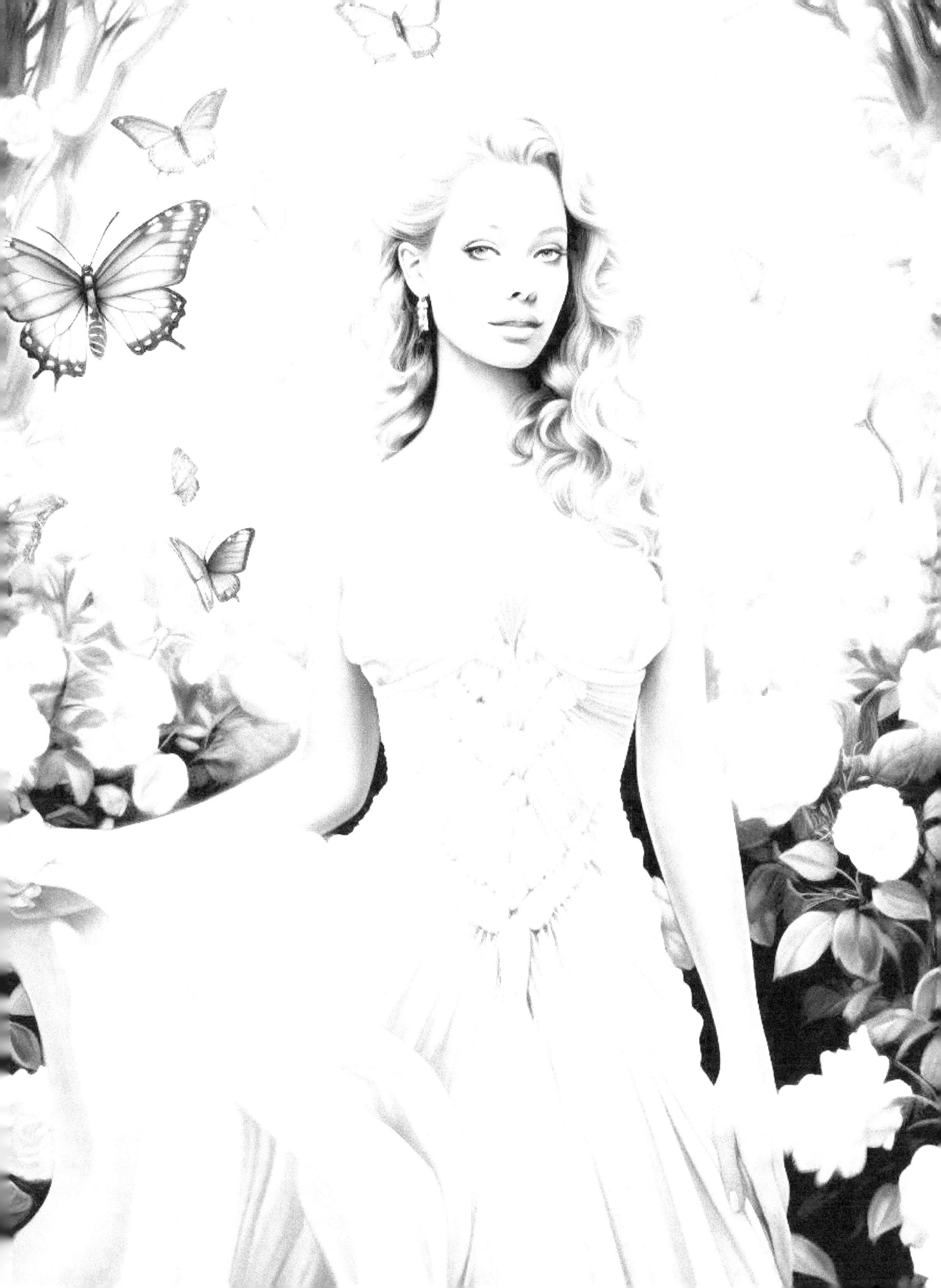

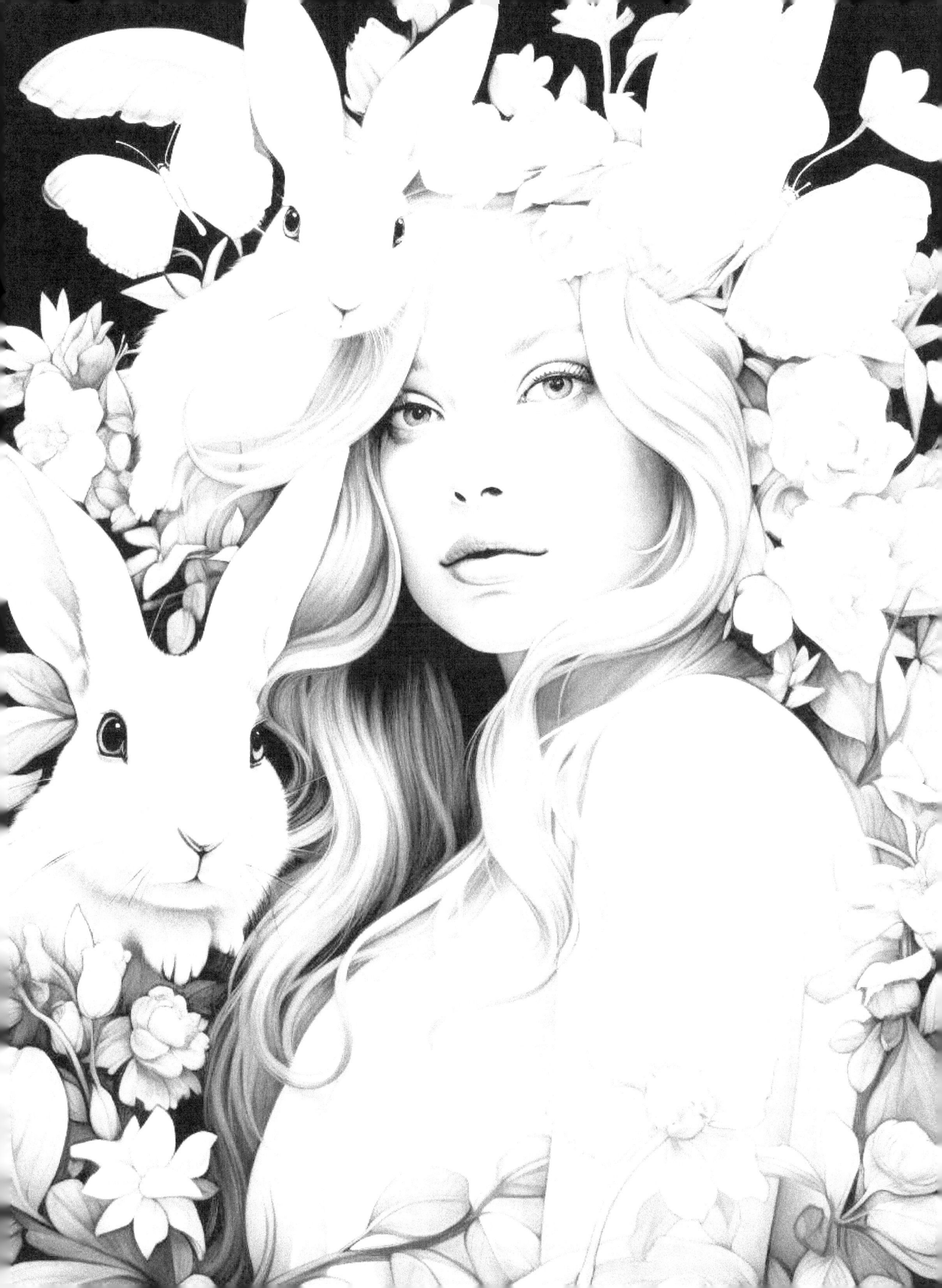

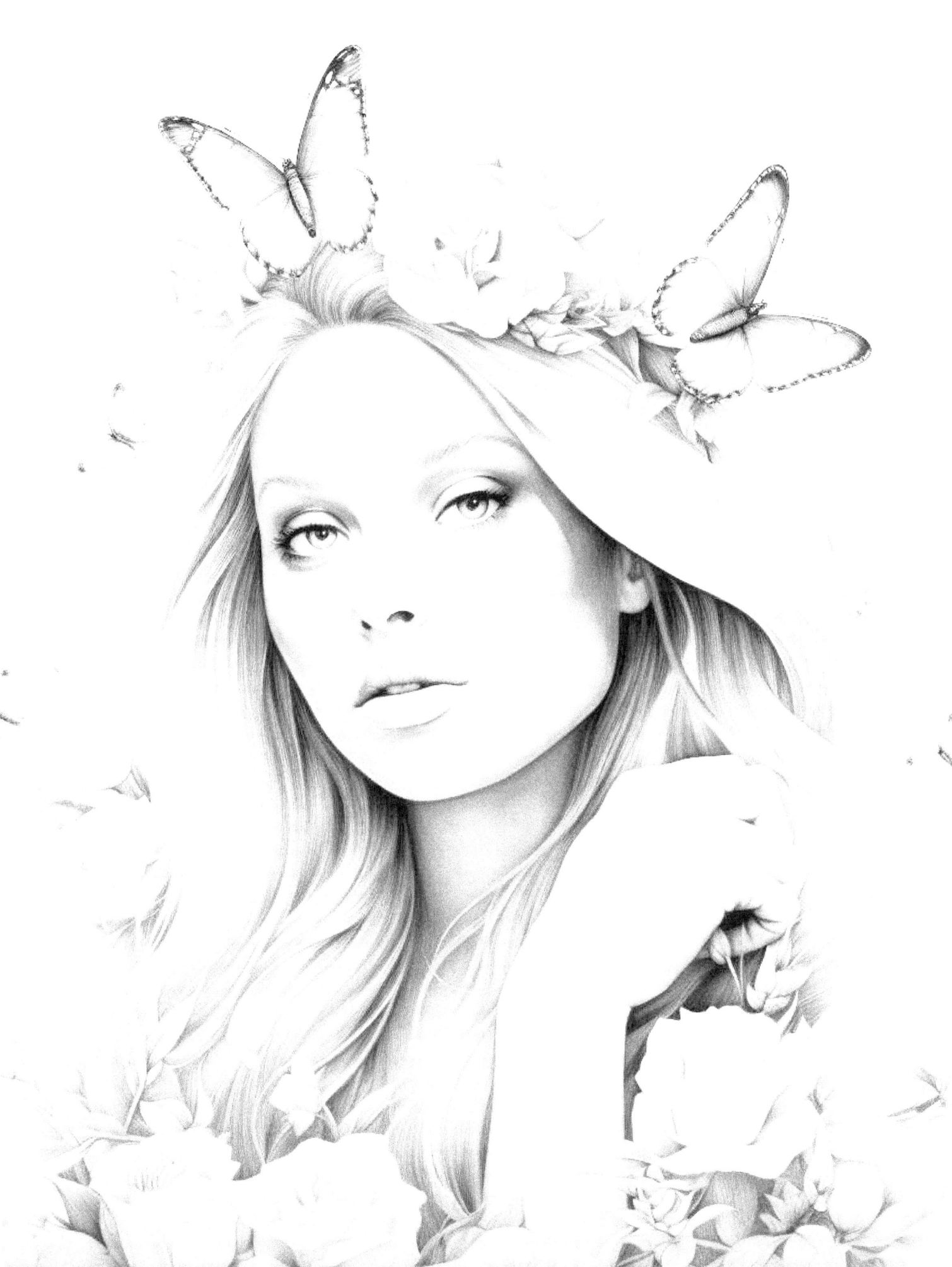

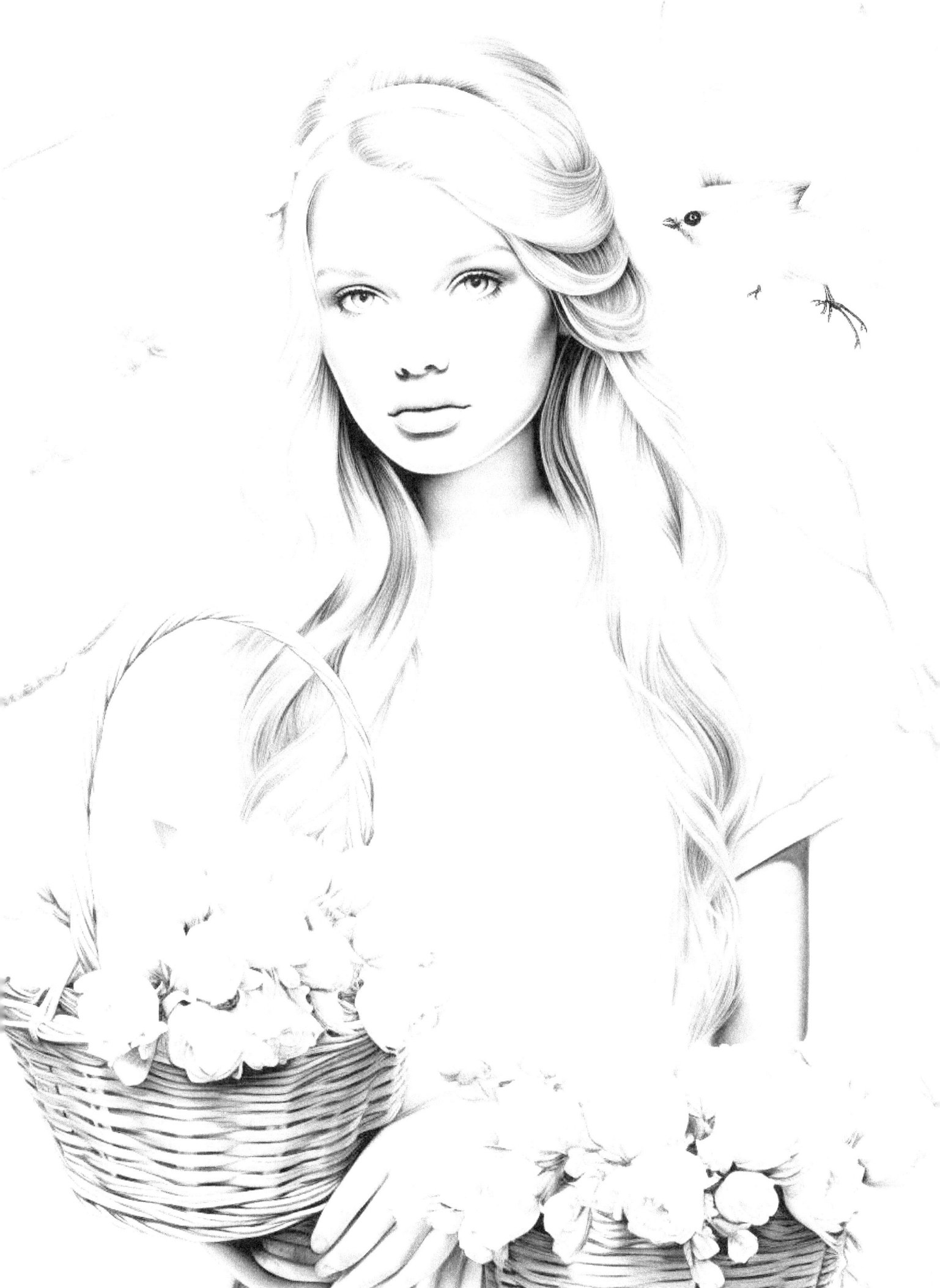

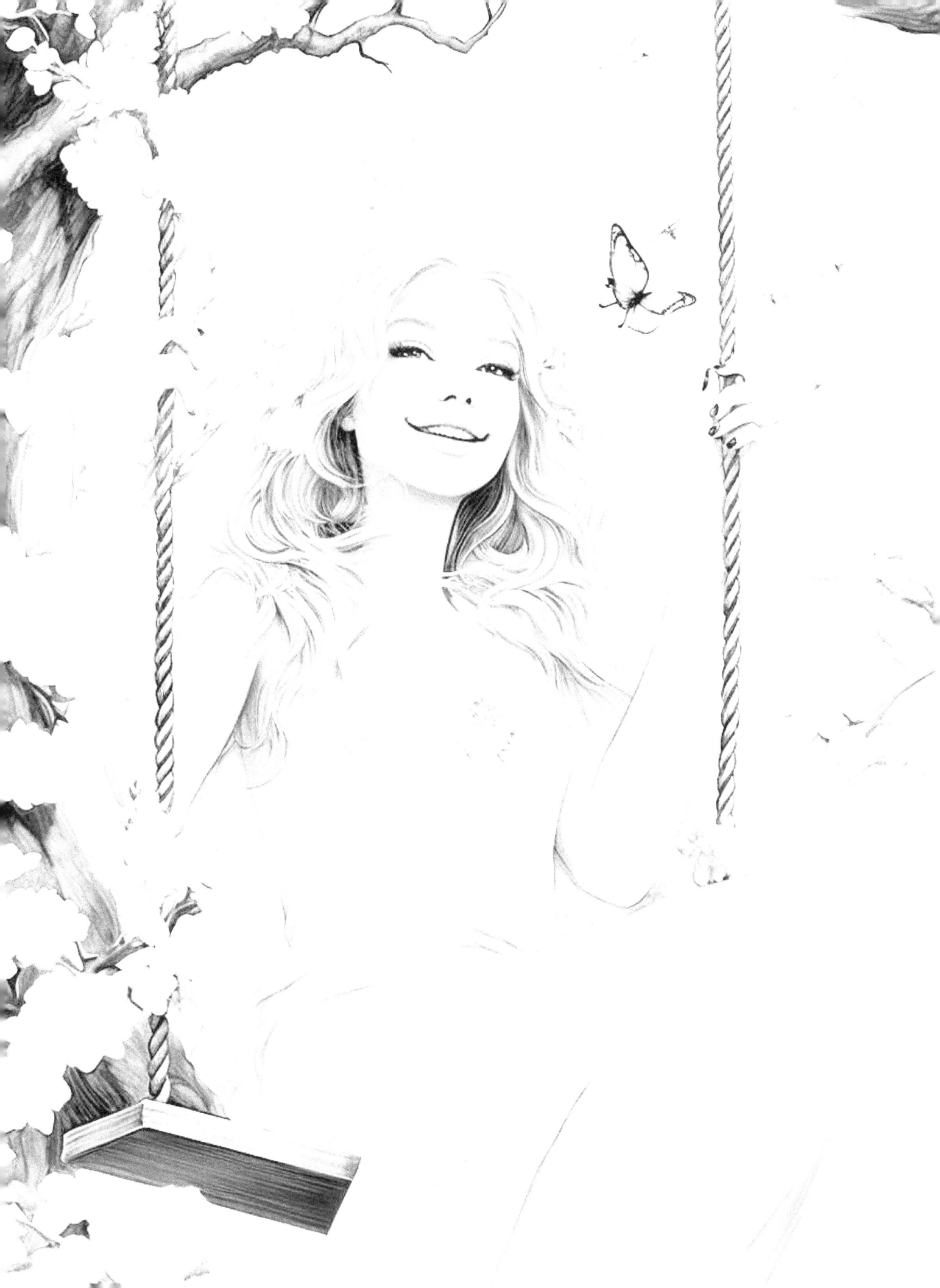

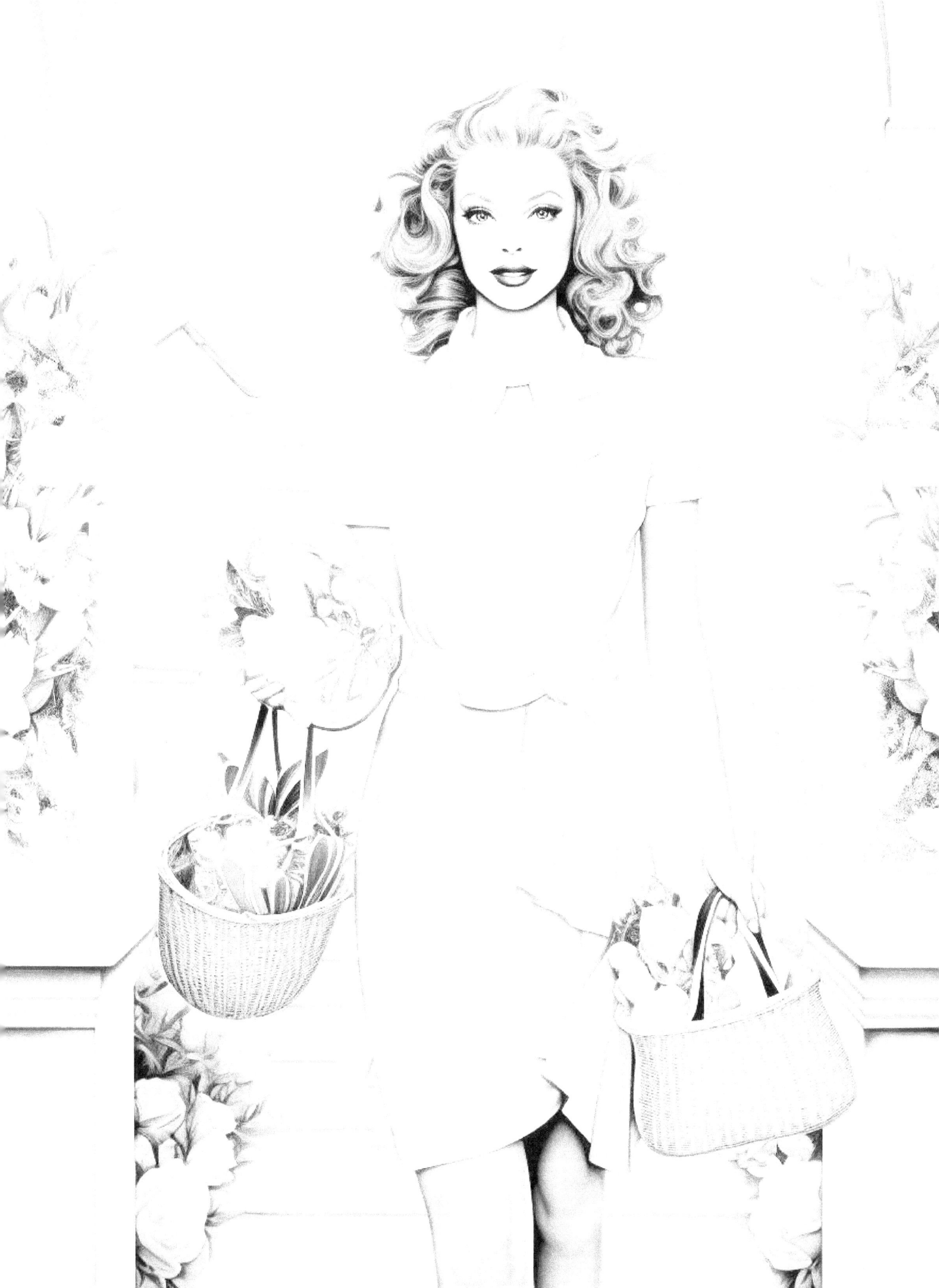

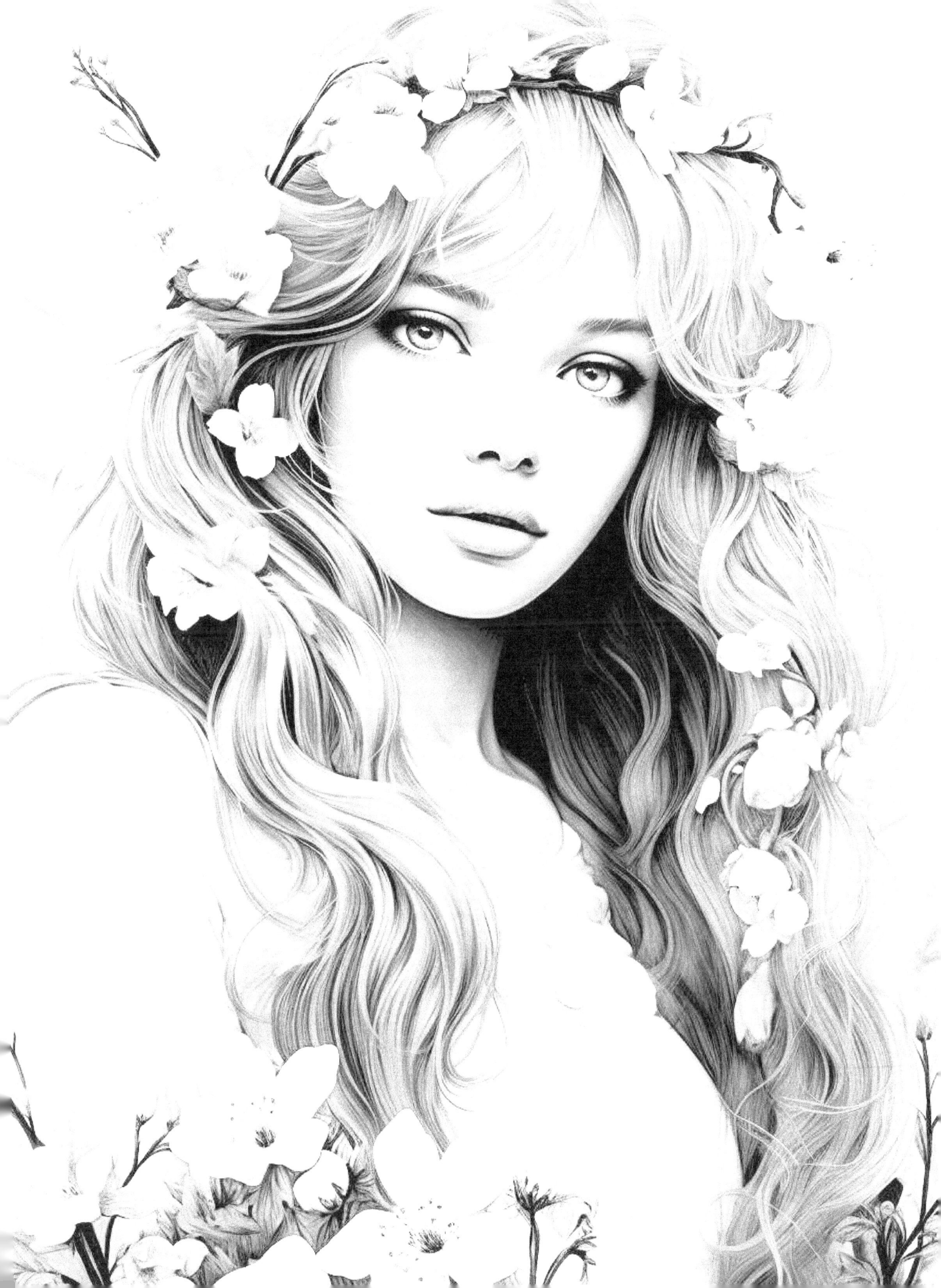

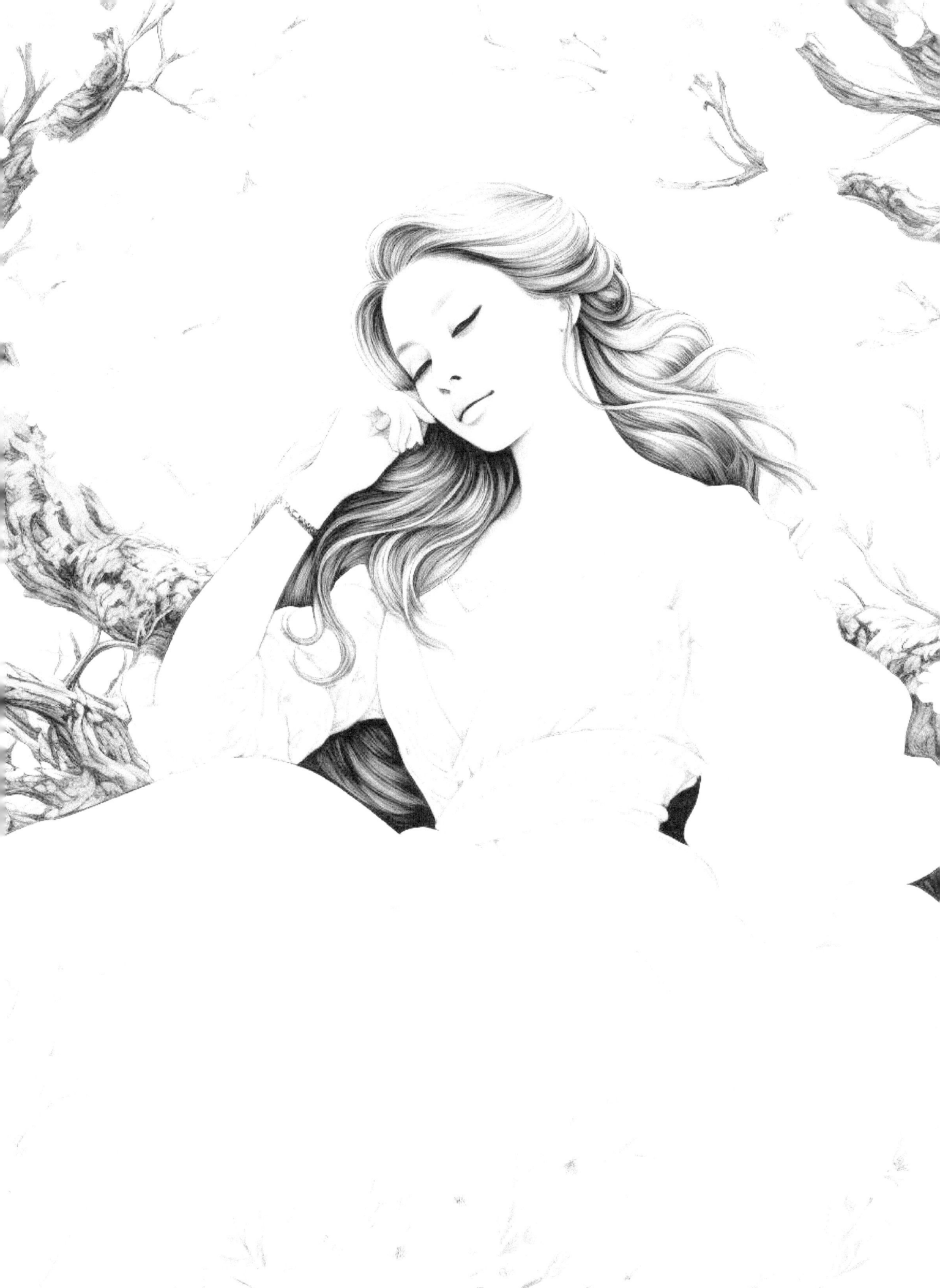

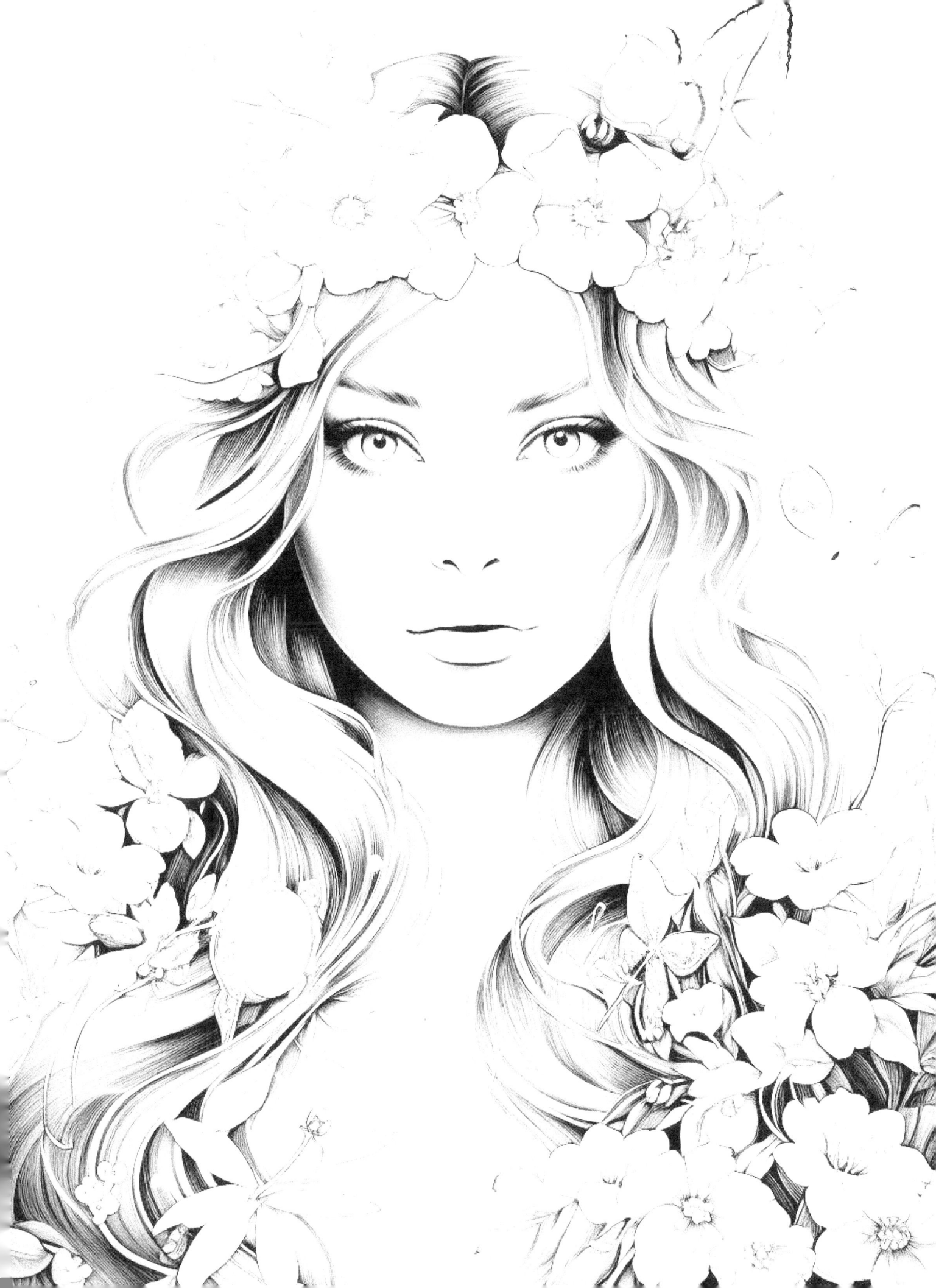

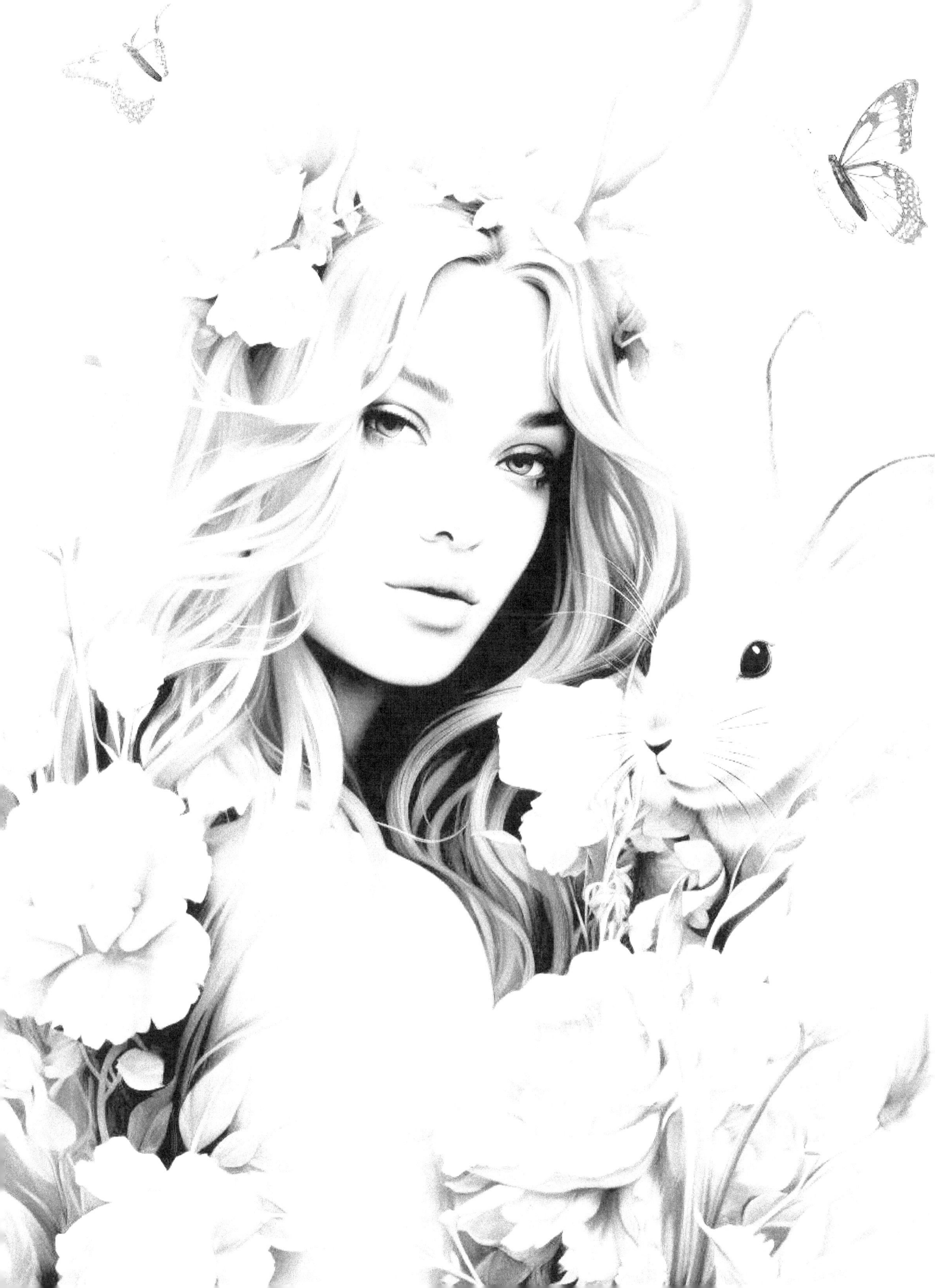

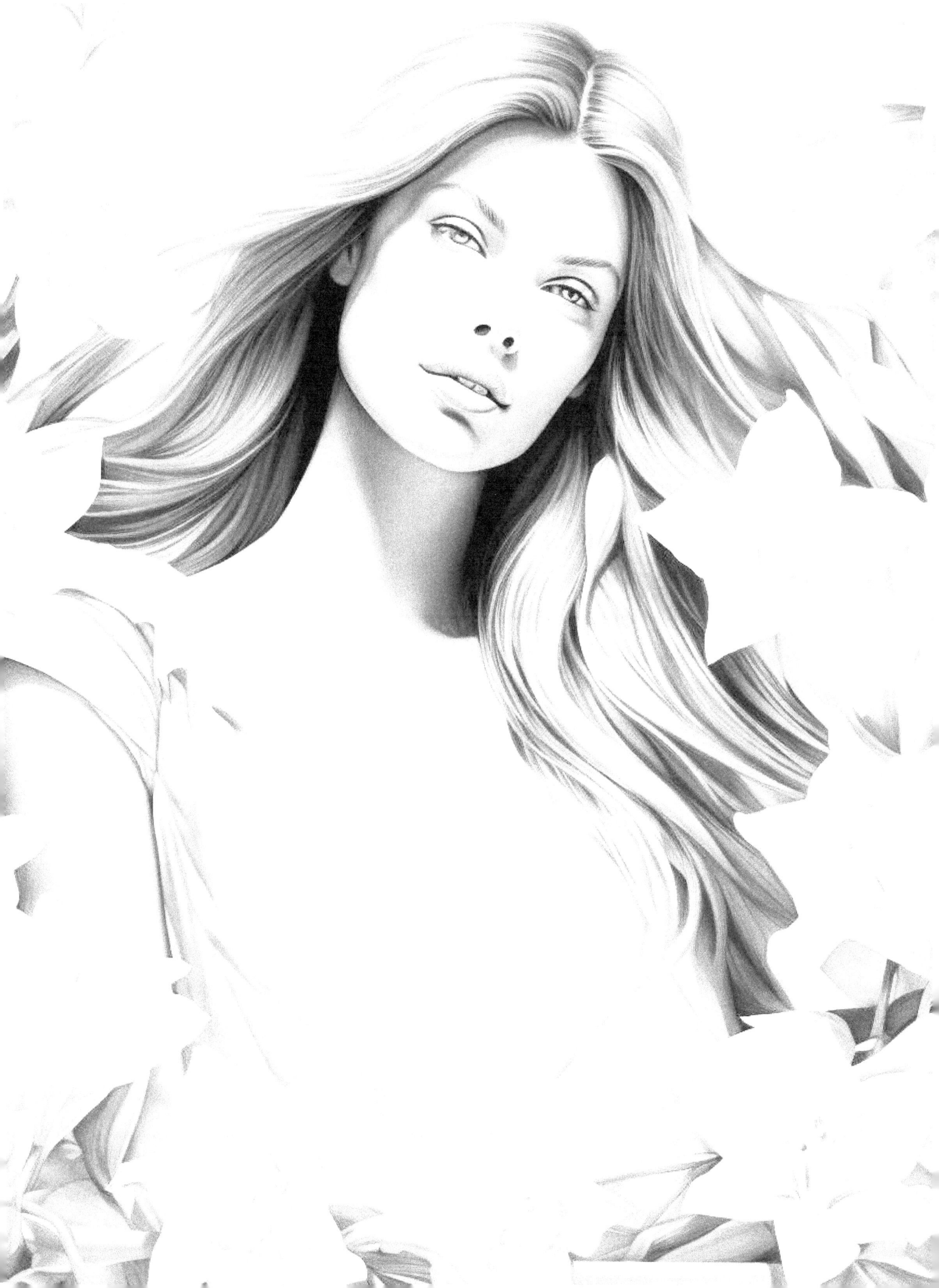

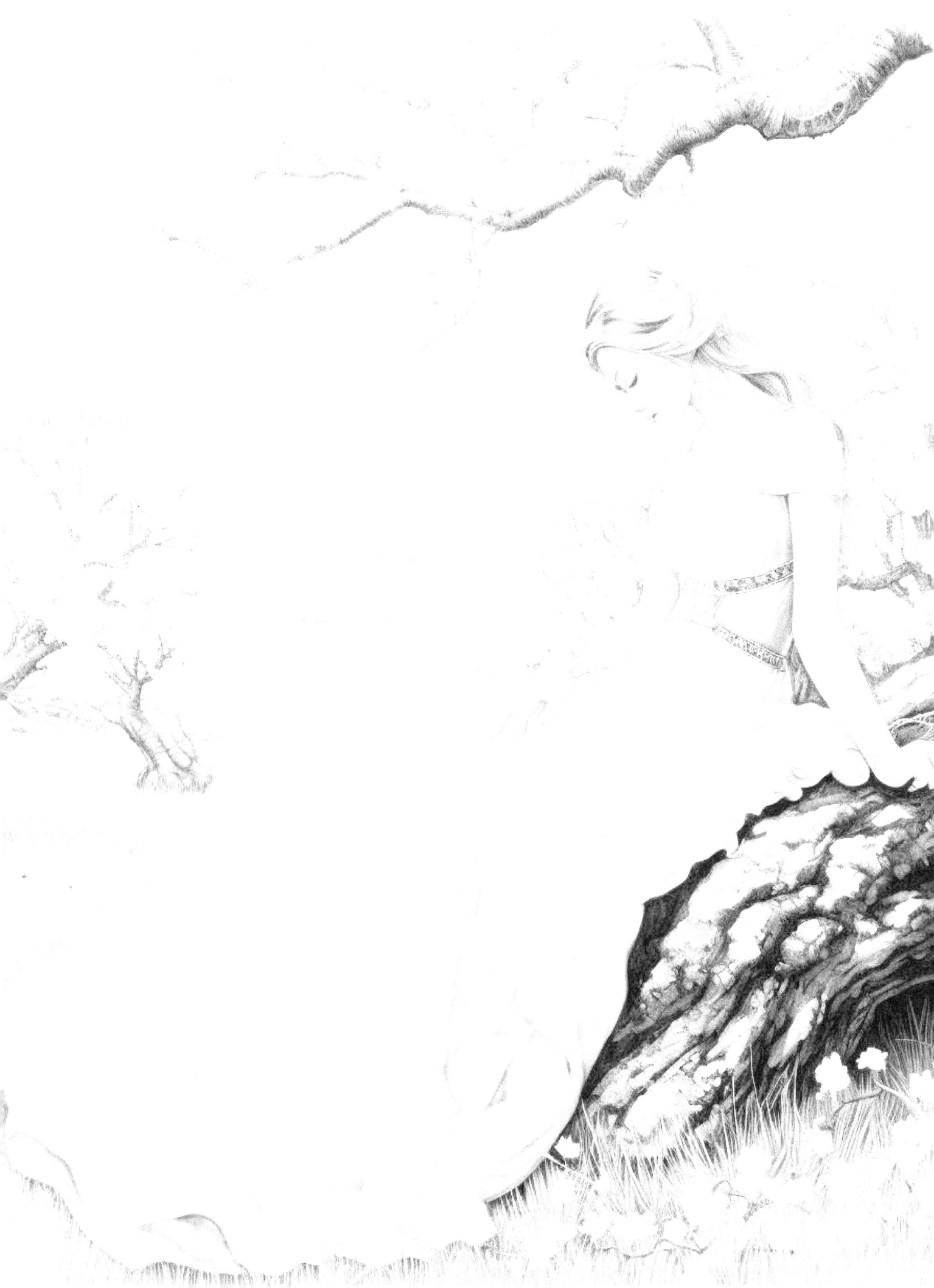

"If you enjoyed our product, it would be greatly appreciated if you could leave a review so others can receive the same benefits you have. Your review will help us see what is and what isn't working so we can serve you better and all our other customers even more."

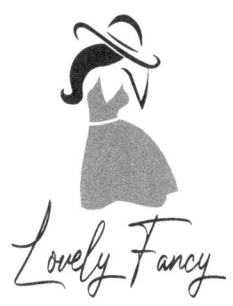

For more beautiful books
Please scan the QR code to access
the Amazon page

Feminine Elegance Across Cultures: A Timeless Portrait Coloring Books

Fantasy Femmes: Pretty Women's Portraits Coloring Journey

www.ingramcontent.com/pod-product-compliance
Lightning Source LLC
Chambersburg PA
CBHW062229220526
45471CB00009B/3405